Shadow Armies

Shadow Armies

Fringe Organizations and
Foot Soldiers of Hindutva

Dhirendra K. Jha

JUGGERNAUT BOOKS
KS House, 118 Shahpur Jat, New Delhi 110049, India

First published in hardback by Juggernaut Books 2017
Published in paperback 2019

Copyright © Dhirendra K. Jha 2017

10 9 8 7 6 5 4 3 2 1

All rights reserved. No part of this publication may be reproduced, transmitted, or stored in a retrieval system in any form or by any means without the written permission of the publisher.

The views and opinions expressed in this book are the author's own. The facts contained herein were reported to be true as on the date of publication by the author to the publishers of the book, and the publishers are not in any way liable for their accuracy or veracity.

ISBN 9789353450199

Typeset in Adobe Caslon Pro by R. Ajith Kumar, New Delhi

Printed at Manipal Technologies Limited, Manipal

Contents

Introduction   1

1. Sanatan Sanstha   9
2. Hindu Yuva Vahini   33
3. Bajrang Dal   59
4. Sri Ram Sene   85
5. Hindu Aikya Vedi   109
6. Abhinav Bharat   135
7. Bhonsala Military School   159
8. Rashtriya Sikh Sangat   187

Notes   211
Acknowledgements   227
A Note on the Author   229

Introduction

India has seen astonishing growth in the politics of Hindutva over the last three decades. Several strands of this brand of politics – not just the Bharatiya Janata Party (BJP) but also those working for it in the shadows – have shot into prominence. They are all fuelled by a single motive: to ensure that one particular community, the Hindus, has the exclusive right to define our national identity. The Rashtriya Swayamsevak Sangh (RSS), a pan-Indian organization comprising chauvinistic Hindu men, is the vanguard of this politics. Formed in 1925, the RSS is not yet a legal entity in so far as it is not registered under any law of the land. Though it claims to be a cultural organization, political motivation has always remained its core concern.

Modelled on the British colonial army, with a similar uniform and training in armed and unarmed combat, and drawing heavily from Benito Mussolini's fascist outfits in Italy, the RSS experienced several ups and downs after Independence. It was banned thrice – first for over a year after the assassination of Mahatma Gandhi in 1948, then for nearly two years during the Emergency in the 1970s, and lastly for a few months in the aftermath of the demolition of the Babri Masjid in 1992 – but its membership has kept growing.

The RSS network, too, has multiplied steadily. At present, the Sangh has roughly three dozen affiliates across the country. Some of the prominent affiliates are its trade union wing, the Bharatiya Mazdoor Sangh; its students union, the Akhil Bharatiya Vidyarthi Parishad (ABVP); its flamboyant cultural outfit, the Vishwa Hindu Parishad (VHP); and the VHP's youth wing, the Bajrang Dal. The RSS and its various offshoots, collectively known as the Sangh Parivar (the Sangh family), run more than 1,50,000 known projects across India, including tribal welfare, educational and Hindu religious programmes apart from innumerable other projects about which we know little or nothing.

Officially, the BJP is the sole RSS outfit given to politics, but in practice most of its affiliates work as political instruments to turn India into a Hindu Rashtra. They do this in the garb of protecting Hinduism. One could argue that the RSS and the VHP are the biggest shadow organizations of the BJP. Except for contesting elections, they do almost everything a political party would do: mobilize masses, develop issues for political polarization, and play a role in identifying electoral candidates and managing booth-level campaigns. Throughout the research for this book, I was struck by the omnipresence of these pan-Indian outfits. The direct or indirect influence of their members was visible in each of the organizations I chose to study.

Though the RSS publicly eschews politics, as the parent body it not only supplies much of the strategic and ideological direction as well as cadres and leaders to the BJP and other associates, but also has its hand – directly or through its affiliates – in several communal conflagrations. It is these attacks on minorities that lead to the kind of polarization necessary for the growth of Hindutva politics.

All this is done in a highly equivocal manner. This equivocation can be found everywhere in the Sangh Parivar: in the relationship between the RSS and the BJP, the BJP and the VHP, the VHP and the Bajrang Dal, the BJP and the Hindu Aikya Vedi (HAV), the BJP and the Rashtriya Sikh Sangat, the RSS and the Bhonsala Military School, etc.

Whenever these other bodies create a controversy, the RSS and the BJP promptly label them 'fringe organizations'. The fact, however, is that they are active parts of the Sangh Parivar, working as buffer organizations for doing the dirty work the BJP and the RSS were once obliged to do themselves. The brazen acts required to create polarization in our society are often carried out by these very establishments.

Some of the 'fringe organizations' seem to exist outside the purview of the Sangh Parivar in so far as they are not technically created and controlled by the RSS. Prominent among them are the Sanatan Sanstha, the Hindu Yuva Vahini, the Sri Ram Sene and the Abhinav Bharat. Yet they are not entirely autonomous. Most of them have an umbilical cord attached to the Sangh Parivar, and all of them are ideologically on the same page. Like the RSS and its affiliates, they claim to derive their ideological raison d'être from V.D. Savarkar's *Hindutva: Who is a Hindu?*

Published in 1923, this tract argues that it is Hindutva (Hindu-ness), rather than Hinduism, that constitutes Hindu identity. According to Savarkar, a Hindu is someone who considers Bharat his holy land, carries the 'blood of the great race' of Vedic people, and claims as his own 'the Hindu Sanskriti'. In practical terms, despite their play of words with regard to their ideology, these organizations – again like the RSS and its offshoots – have interlocked 'Hindutva' and 'Hinduism', becoming in the end a manifestation of hatred towards minority religious groups, especially Muslims, Christians and Sikhs.

The portrayal of Muslims in particular as threats to Hindus – thus justifying the constant attacks on them – has remained the single most important tool of all branches of Hindutva politics. Though the practitioners would never say this in public, the objective of these activities is always the same: to create a false fear among

Introduction

Hindus and stoke the polarization of their votes in favour of the party leading the forces of Hindutva.

In the case of the Sikhs, however, persuasion replaces confrontation. The motive of the Sangh Parivar is to kill Sikh identity and amalgamate Sikhism as part of Hinduism. Sikhs are not in the category of the 'threatening other'; they face Hindutva wrath only when they stress on an identity separate from the Hindus.

At first glance, these fringe organizations – whether part of the Sangh Parivar or working independently – often seem to reflect the ups and downs of local or regional politics. A deeper look, however, would show them as communal eddies generated by the powerful currents of Hindutva politics. The BJP's political evolution from two seats in the Lok Sabha in 1984 to 282 seats in 2014, constituting an absolute majority in the Lower House of Parliament, is not a journey of just one political party – it is also the journey of its myriad shadow armies.

Yet, there is little insight into the actual mechanisms that underlie the evolution of these fringe outfits. We do not have a systematic understanding of how they work and how they connect with licit politics. These shadow armies are not direct projections of their pan-Indian partner. Each of them possesses a distinct identity. This book is an attempt to find out the when, the how and the why of these organizations.

For a long time, I thought they primarily act as

recruiting and training centres for their brethren who officially practise politics. This was because I looked at them through the prism of pan-Indian Hindutva organizations like the RSS, the BJP and the VHP. It struck me only when I began to travel for research and talk to people that these fringe organizations could have their own paths of evolution, beset by internal contradictions and driven by local anxieties and motivations.

Of the eight organizations I chose to research, four belong to the Sangh Parivar and four operate independently. While the former set includes the Bajrang Dal, the Rashtriya Sikh Sangat, the Bhonsala Military School and the Hindu Aikya Vedi, the latter group constitutes the Sanatan Sanstha, the Hindu Yuva Vahini, the Sri Ram Sene and the Abhinav Bharat.

From Uttar Pradesh and Bihar, regions which I knew well, I embarked on a journey through western, central, southern and eastern India in an attempt to trace the history of the growth of these outfits. In my travels, I met fascinating characters. Some were intelligent, some dumb, and a few even criminals looking for political cover, but they were all full of vitality and vigour and quite aware of what they were doing. Through their narratives they led me to the actual working of the ideology of their hydra-like network.

The term Hindutva – explained by Savarkar as 'Hindu-ness' and not 'Hinduism' – is almost always used to refer to the core idea at the heart of the members of the Sangh

Introduction

Parivar. But on the ground, it is easy to get misled if one does not reverse the meaning of this term. It is Hinduism that is invoked to ensure the mobilization of masses and the polarization of voters. Hindutva as an ideological construct simply vanishes the moment one leaves the national headquarters of the BJP and the RSS.

The irony is that the young men from backward or lower castes who constitute a significant portion of the foot soldiers of these shadow armies are rarely able to recognize that the Hindutva to which they have dedicated their energies is nothing but brahminism. And that it is the same brahminical Hinduism that has kept them oppressed for centuries and against which they have their own legacies of resistance. They are so blinded by their growing Hindu religiosity and hatred for the 'threatening other' that they simply cannot see how the Hindutva they are working for ultimately seeks to revive the historical hegemony of brahmins and other upper castes.

Occasionally, the truth becomes visible. For instance, when caste hierarchies affect the distribution of power even at the local level. Sometimes this leads to the revolt of backward caste leaders and cadres (as in the case of the Sri Ram Sene), but the rebels hardly ever look for an ideological alternative.

The triumph of Hindutva, following the BJP's striking victory in the 2014 Lok Sabha elections and in many of the state polls thereafter, has resulted in brahminism trying to recolonize the spaces it had been forced to vacate due to social reform movements and anti-brahminical ideological struggles. In the chapters that follow I only offer vignettes illustrating how the shadow world of Hindutva, with its reliance on violence, hate speech and even terror, has contributed to these electoral triumphs as well as to the brahminical agenda underpinning the overall Hindu nationalist project.

Note: A large part of the argument of this book is based on field work done in the states of Uttar Pradesh, Bihar, Odisha, Madhya Pradesh, Punjab, Gujarat, Maharashtra, Goa, Karnataka and Kerala. The archival material dug out from Delhi, Mumbai, Pune, Thiruvananthapuram, Lucknow, Gorakhpur and Amritsar helped in understanding the historical contexts within which these Hindutva organizations assume form.

1
Sanatan Sanstha

I

Picture a palatial china-white mansion with a massive porch amidst the lush green of a Goan village. Guards in slick blue uniform stand in patrol at its entrance. This is the Sanatan Sanstha's ashram at Ramnathi, where the organization's self-styled 'God', Dr Jayant Balaji Athavale, lives. The three-storey building appears to have been designed to strike awe among the villagers, but it is resentment and revulsion that one sees in their eyes every time you mention the ashram.

Every morning over a hundred visitors stream in – mostly young men and women in the Sanstha's saffron attire with a vermilion mark on their foreheads. Disciples of Athavale, they stay inside the ashram for the whole day with the permanent residents – who also number around a hundred – and go back to their accommodations outside the village late in the evening.

Across the road, opposite the mansion, a wide open field slopes down to a rivulet that forms the northern boundary of the village. Until recently, the land had yielded bountiful crops every agricultural season. But one day, early in the monsoon of 2008, a powerful stink arose as the logged water receded from the field. 'The smell was so foul that it soon became unbearable. The villagers came out of their houses to an appalling sight – the receded water had left behind hundreds and thousands of used condoms that covered almost the entire field, making it stink like hell,' says Basant Bhatt, the priest of the illustrious Ramnath Temple at the heart of the village. 'No tiller has ever sought to clean the field and cultivate it again.'[1] The locals found it disgusting. Though the source of the condoms remains a mystery, the blame is firmly placed on the ashram.

The villagers probably arrived at that conclusion because Athavale and his saffron-clad followers had been marked by controversy ever since they arrived in 2002. The Sanstha had tried to construct its ashram in the neighbouring village of Parvatiwada two years before their entry into Ramnathi but the locals there were able to mount a successful resistance. 'It was only after their failure in Parvatiwada that they moved on to Ramnathi, where they succeeded in setting up their ashram,' says Sheker Naik, a senior resident of Parvatiwada and a former sarpanch (2002–04) of the Bandora Panchayat to which both villages belong.[2]

Many people in Ramnathi suspected the Sanatan Sanstha of being some kind of sex cult though there was no evidence of that. The condoms in the field, however, confirmed their misgivings even as the Sanstha refuted the allegations. There was, thus, already a good deal of ill-feeling when on the evening of 16 October 2009, a few hours after a bomb blast at Madgaon, the Goa police swooped in on the Sanstha's ashram at Ramnathi.

As per police records, the Sanstha had opposed the Narkasura effigy contest, a hugely popular festive activity in Goa which takes place on the eve of Diwali. On this day in 2009, 16 October, two Sanstha members – Malgonda Patil and Yogesh Naik – were allegedly carrying a bomb on their scooter to plant near the venue of the contest in Madgaon. However, the bomb went off prematurely and the duo died.[3]

'We were shocked,' recounts Saurabh Lotlikar, a social worker and a resident of Ramnathi. 'That very day some of the villagers got together and formed a public interest group, Jan Jagruti Manch, with Basant Bhatt as the president and Sheker Naik the secretary. Its sole objective was to fight for the removal of the Sanatan Sanstha from the village.'[4]

The new group called a meeting the very next day. Only a handful of locals participated. 'But we persisted, and day after day the knot of people around us grew bigger. Then we called a public meeting on 20 October. That meeting was massive. People not just from Ramnathi but from the entire Ponda subdivision turned up in large numbers,' says Basant Bhatt. 'We did not expect more than three or four hundred people, but nearly two thousand participated. Later we also organized a march against the Sanatan Sanstha and that, too, was attended by a large number of people.'

The demonstrations in Ramnathi put the Sanstha on the back foot for a while. The local press covered the agitation comprehensively, with two to three pieces on the subject appearing almost every day for many weeks. But these stories put together yield little information about the nature of the Sanatan Sanstha or the substance of Athavale's preaching.

II

Until the Madgaon blast, despite viewing the Sanstha with hostility, the villagers did not see it as a powerful and dangerous group that would stop at nothing to achieve its own, possibly sinister, ends. They were not aware, for example, that the blast was not the first such act it had effected or that the Sanstha's members had also been involved in previous blasts.

In mid 2008, the Maharashtra police had arrested several Sanstha members for setting off bombs in Thane and Vashi. On 4 June, a bomb had exploded in the parking area of the Gadkari Rangayatan Auditorium in Thane, injuring seven people. The Sanstha members were ostensibly protesting the Marathi play *Amhi Pachpute*, which they claimed showed Hindu gods and goddesses in a poor light. A few days earlier, on 31 May, a low intensity bomb had gone off at the Vishnudas Bhave Auditorium in Vashi. In August 2011, a Mumbai court sentenced two members of the Sanstha – Vikram Bhave and Ramesh

Gadkari – to ten years' rigorous imprisonment for the Thane and Vashi blasts.[5]

The Sanstha's response in all these cases was to disown its members as soon as they were arrested and simply refuse to take any responsibility for their activities. It followed this strategy despite the Goa police unravelling the true story of the Sanstha within a few months of the Madgaon explosion. 'At present the institution [Sanatan Sanstha] appears to be developing into a stage of terror activities,' says a Goa police report prepared in 2010, 'and if allowed to grow up in a peaceful state, there is eminent danger to the life, property, communal harmony of the state and the nation.'[6] This report formed the basis of a thousand-page dossier seeking a ban on the Sanstha submitted by the Maharashtra Anti-Terrorism Squad (ATS) to the Union Home Ministry in 2011. The entire exercise, however, was futile as a difference of opinion developed between the state and central governments, and no action was taken against the Sanstha.

It is not clear whether Prithviraj Chavan, who was the chief minister of Maharashtra, did not pursue the matter seriously or Union Home Minister Sushil Kumar Shinde developed cold feet about banning the Sanstha. Four years later, in 2015, when the BJP had replaced the Congress both at the centre and in the state, and a chorus seeking a ban erupted once again, Shinde blamed Chavan for showing a 'lack of seriousness' on the matter. To this the latter retorted, 'I'm hurt by what my senior party colleague has said. I should not be commenting on it, but it [Shinde's comment] is laughable.'

On paper, the Sanatan Sanstha was originally registered as a charitable trust under the name 'Sanatan Bharatiya Sanskruti Sanstha' at Mumbai in 1991. It claimed to be established 'to educate people about the science of spiritualism' by organizing discourses, seminars, workshops, etc. 'to encourage people to be seekers' and 'to guide seekers until they meet their Guru'.[7] Dr Jayant Balaji Athavale, the Guru, signed the deed as one of the four trustees. The others who signed with him were his wife, Dr Kunda Jayant Athavale, and his followers Vijay Neelkantha Bhave and Vinay Neelkantha Bhave.

The nebulousness of the whole enterprise is further emphasized by the fact that several other outfits sprang up in course of time – all owing allegiance to Athavale yet presenting themselves as independent entities and not the Sanstha's affiliates. The Sanatan Sanstha, for instance, was registered much later in Goa with its office at 'Sanatan Ashram, Ramnathi, Ponda, Goa'. Other ashrams of the Sanstha, like those at Panvel and Meraj in Maharashtra, were registered as separate trusts; so were organizations like the Hindu Janajagruti Samiti and the Dharmashakti Sena as well as the newspaper *Sanatan Prabhat*.

The Sanstha and all of Athavale's 'independent' entities do everything to show they are a rarefied group given essentially to spiritualism. Athavale's disciples (known as sadhaks and sadhikas) start their day at 6 a.m.

with meditation and prayers that go on for two hours, followed by a vegetarian breakfast. Then they read the *Sanatan Prabhat*, through which Athavale – who has been bedridden since 2013 and meets with only a small group of close aides – is known to communicate with them. Thereafter, they perform seva in various sections of the ashram. This includes working on the publication of holy texts in Marathi, English, Hindi, Kannada and a few other languages; designing idols and pictures of deities; preparing almanacs which are published annually in eight languages; making short films on how to impart education on Dharma and how to celebrate festivals; writing for and editing the *Sanatan Prabhat*; managing various Sanstha-related websites; and training priests to impart the knowledge of Dharma to society.

The branding of the other outfits as 'independent' is probably meant to protect Athavale in case any of them is caught red-handed and charged with illegal activity. It is not inconceivable that Athavale has considered the legal advantage of creating a network of outfits instead of setting up branches under the aegis of a parent body. In any case, 'Athavaleism' appears to be a construct that runs straight into the face of the Indian Constitution. His spiritual teachings may often appear harmless but his political teachings are far from benign. Many editions of the *Sanatan Prabhat* have proclaimed that the organization aims to establish a 'Hindu Rashtra' by 2023. Its articles and headlines attack Muslims, Christians, rationalists and communists on a regular basis and dub them as evil-doers. In 2007, the *Sanatan Prabhat* quoted Athavale: 'You feel so victorious after killing a mosquito, imagine how you would feel after killing an evil person?'[8] On 29 February 2008 the paper asked Athavale's followers not to damage buses and private vehicles, and act instead like Maoists against the arrogant police force. It also published a mobile number as a contact point to organize training for the purpose.[9]

III

If Athavale's views have shocked and repelled many people, they have also attracted others, principally groups of upper-caste young Hindus in western Maharashtra who are ostensibly driven by their desire to turn India into a Hindu Rashtra.

Athavale began his career as a clinical hypnotherapist, practising in Britain during the 1970s. In the late 1980s, he set up a hypnosis clinic in Mumbai's Sion (West) locality where he began organizing workshops on spirituality. During this period he and his wife Kunda Athavale forged relations with various spiritual gurus and groups and began delivering lectures on the 'science of spiritualism'.

After registering the Sanatan Bharatiya Sanskruti Sanstha in 1991, he began to hold meditation camps for lay followers of the spiritual gurus and groups with whom he had formed ties. He also published a number of books in several languages. In these books and his preachings, he stressed that the most important task for a sadhak was to find and reach God and His truth. In order to achieve that a sadhak must completely surrender to the Guru whose will had to be followed strictly and unquestioningly. Athavale publicly announced that the objective of his movement was to establish 'Ishwary Rajya' (the Kingdom of God) on earth by destroying 'durjans' (evil forces), who indulged in 'bad habits', 'bad politics, economy and culture', and 'misinterpreted religious beliefs', so on and so forth.

The Sanstha's 'self-defence training' manuals teach its members how to fire a gun. They also say that while shooting 'the gaze should be towards durjans'. A survey of the Sanstha's literature and illustrations makes it obvious that 'durjan' implies rationalists, Muslims, Christians and anyone perceived as anti-Hindu.

According to *Kshatradharma Sadhana*, one of the manuals compiled by Athavale, 'Five per cent of seekers will need to undergo training with weapons. The Lord will provide the weapons at the opportune moment through some medium.' The manual also says, 'It does not matter if one is not used to shooting. When he shoots along with chanting the Lord's name the bullet certainly strikes the target due to the inherent power in the Lord's name.'

Around the mid 1990s, once Athavale had a substantial number of sadhaks, he developed a proper curriculum for the Sanstha's meditation camps and satsangs. Sadhaks who are trained thus travel to new areas to organize similar camps and satsangs. In these camps sadhaks are encouraged to narrate their 'anubhutis' (experiences), with the special ones being sent to Athavale, the Guru, for interpretation. These anubhutis are also published in the *Sanatan Prabhat* which every sadhak has to read as part of his daily routine. This, along with discussions on items on religion and nation published in the Sanstha's newspaper, is treated as part of the sadhana.

Athavale, as the Ishwary Avatar (divine incarnation) having taken birth to establish Ishwary Rajya, marks – in percentage points – the progress of a sadhak in his sadhana. It is believed in the Sanstha that once a sadhak's progress moves past the 80 per cent mark, he becomes a 'sant'. Athavale alone can decide whether this threshold has been crossed. Sainthood gives a sadhak an exalted position and brings him a lot of privileges in the community. 'His Holiness' (or simply 'HH') gets affixed to his name, and he is treated with veneration by Athavale's followers. His status is announced formally in the *Sanatan Prabhat*. Sainthood is the highest dream that every sadhak or sadhika is said to nurture in the Sanstha because it is with these saints acting as lieutenants that Athavale will establish the promised Ishwary Rajya.

Of late, Athavale himself seems to have undergone an exercise to elevate his own status in the commune – from that of a Guru to a God. This has been achieved by means of the 'divine changes' that have taken place 'over the years' in his body. The miraculous transformation was declared on the Sanstha's various websites and blogs in 2015. 'Over the years, there have been many changes on HH Dr Athavale's body both due to negative energy attacks and due to a gross manifestation of His Divinity,' reports an article that appeared in the *Indian Express* in September 2015, referring to the Sanstha's websites.[10] Some of the specific changes listed on these websites were: Athavale's hair turning golden; divine particles falling from his body; the symbol of Om appearing on his fingernails, forehead and tongue; and various fragrances emanating from his body.[11] A post on one of the Sanstha's blogs referred to him as God.

'Guru (Dr) Athavale, who is striving day and night to achieve the lofty ideal of establishing Hindu Nation, is the personification of God. […] Maharshis have recently declared that He is the Incarnation of Shri Vishnu. Even from the Divine changes in His body and the Divine auspicious signs appearing on his body, it is proved that He is not an ordinary human being, but God Himself.'[12]

What these beliefs and doctrines have meant as a matter of practice is difficult to tell as sadhaks have been making a deliberate effort to rebut charges by the administration and the critics that they are 'a sex commune' spreading 'extreme forms of superstition' and turning fast into 'an exceptionally dangerous cult'.

In Maharashtra, which has a rich tradition of

progressive movements, the Sanstha came into conflict with the rationalists early on. The latter questioned its beliefs and doctrines and criticized Athavale and his group of sadhaks – along with other obscurantist forces in the state – for spreading superstition through manipulative pseudo-spiritual practices. The hostility between the Sanstha and the rationalists initially took the shape of regular showdowns, with the former organizing attacks on programmes and workshops conducted by the rationalists and the latter openly challenging sadhaks to demonstrate their 'miracles' in full public view.

Then the hostilities took a dangerous turn.

IV

In 2013, a spate of brutal high-profile assassinations struck Maharashtra and Karnataka, leading to the arrest of the Sanstha's sadhaks. The first to be killed was Dr Narendra Dabholkar, the leading face of Maharashtra's rationalist movement. He had set up the Maharashtra Andhashraddha Nirmoolan Samiti (MANS) in 1989, shortly before Athavale registered the Sanatan Bharatiya Sanskruti Sanstha, his first trust. As the two organizations grew, so did the conflicts between them. By the turn of the century, MANS and Dabholkar, a medical doctor by training, became the foremost champion of the anti-superstition bill, which the state government left hanging for more than a decade.

'Promoting rationalism and scientific temper was the central point of Dabholkar's whole effort,' said Rahul Thorat, managing editor of MANS's newsletter, *Andhashraddha Nirmoolan Vartapatra*.[13] 'He was sure that superstitions arising from one's ignorance can be eradicated very easily once the reasoning and trickery behind them are explained.'

In 1999, Dabholkar prepared a draft anti-superstition bill and launched a relentless campaign for its enactment. To force the government to pass it, he experimented with a range of non-violent and peaceful methods – holding demonstrations, courting arrest and organizing large-scale letter campaigns.

The Sanstha mounted a counter campaign against the bill. Its contention was that if the legislation was passed, Hindus wouldn't be allowed to perform pujas in their homes. The Shiv Sena, the BJP and a whole lot of Hindu religious groups joined hands with the Sanstha to oppose the bill.

In the early hours of 20 August 2013, when the MANS's movement for the anti-superstition law was at its peak, Dabholkar was gunned down by two men near the Omkareshwar Temple in Pune while out on a morning walk. The assailants fired three rounds at him from point-blank range and fled on a bike parked nearby. Dabholkar received one bullet in the head and died instantly. He had faced several threats and assaults during his lifetime but had always rejected police protection, saying: 'If I have to take police protection in my own country from my own people, then there is something wrong with me. I'm fighting within the framework of the Indian Constitution and it is not against anyone, but for everyone.'

The popular outrage that followed the assassination of Dabholkar forced the government to act swiftly on the anti-superstition law. An ordinance was issued soon after the murder, and in December that year, the state legislature passed the Maharashtra Prevention and Eradication of Human Sacrifice and Other Inhuman, Evil and Aghori Practices and Black Magic Act, 2013. Many rationalists, however, feel the Act is a watered-down version of Dabholkar's original draft prepared in 1999.

Exactly two years later, almost in a replay of Dabholkar's murder, another prominent rationalist and senior leader of the Communist Party of India (CPI), Govind Pansare, fell victim to an assassin's bullet. Pansare, like Dabholkar, had been at loggerheads with the Sanstha, which had even filed a defamation case against him. A friend of the MANS founder, the CPI leader too had abstained from taking police protection despite receiving death threats. A letter sent to him merely a few months after Dabholkar's murder had issued a clear-cut warning: 'Tumcha Dabholkar karen' (You will meet the fate of Dabholkar).

An indefatigable fighter, Pansare had continued his campaign against communal, superstitious and obscurantist forces. One particular issue which seemed to have angered the conservative sections in Maharashtra the most was his interpretation of Shivaji, the medieval ruler presented by Maharashtra's brahminical chauvinists as an anti-Muslim king who saved Hindus from getting forcibly circumcised and converted to Islam at the hands of Muslim invaders. In his painstakingly researched book *Shivaji Kon Hota?* (Who Was Shivaji?) Pansare demonstrated that Shivaji respected all religions. The book, which went into several reprints and was translated into eight languages, also highlights the fact that one-third of Shivaji's army as well as many of his bodyguards, commanders and even his secretary were all Muslims. It goes on to assert that Shivaji cared for the welfare of his rayyat (tillers of the soil) and had reduced their tax burden. Shivaji's respect for women also stands out clearly in Pansare's writing on the Maratha king.

In one of his widely read articles, 'What should be the Approach of Revolutionaries to Religion', Pansare argues:

> We are living in a world where religious forces, overpowering the views and practices advocated by Gautam Buddha [and] saint reformers like Phule, V.R. Shinde, Agarkar, Mahatma Gandhi, Sane Guruji, Dr Ambedkar and Rajarshi Shahu, have generated a beastly fundamentalist frenzy and captured power. Our task is cut out before us. It is to win back those who are deceived by them in order to defeat these forces.[14]

The CPI leader worked tirelessly, delivering lectures in colleges on Shivaji and the social reformers of Maharashtra, publishing booklets and pamphlets, organizing literary events and arguing against superstition.[15] This campaign, however, ended abruptly on 16 February 2015 when Pansare was shot five times by two men on a motorbike while on a morning walk with his wife Uma. Three of the bullets hit him, and his wife suffered a head injury when the gunmen pushed her down before fleeing. Four days later, on 20 February, Pansare succumbed to his wounds.

The pattern of murder was repeated for a third time at Dharwad in Karnataka during the morning of 30 August 2015, when two men on a motorbike came to the residence of M.M. Kalburgi – a veteran Kannada writer known for his strong stand against superstitious practices and right-wing Hindutva groups – and fired two rounds on him at point-blank range before fleeing the scene. An ambulance was called and attempts were made to resuscitate Kalburgi. He was first rushed to a private hospital and from there to the District Civil Hospital of Dharwad, where he was declared brought dead.

Kalburgi, a former vice chancellor of Hampi University, was a scholar of the Lingayat tradition. He was a prominent rationalist in the region who supported eminent Karnataka littérateur U.R. Ananthamurthy, known for his critique of brahmin orthodoxy and communal politics. In a 2014 seminar on the anti-superstition bill in Bengaluru, he had argued fiercely against idolatry. The ferocity of the response of Hindutva groups forced Kalburgi to demand police protection. However, only a few days before his murder he reportedly asked for it to be withdrawn.[16]

It is not only the manner of their murders that links Dabholkar, Pansare and Kalburgi. The three rationalists were also similarly dedicated in their energetic fight against communal and obscurantist forces. Whether they were killed by the same set of people is yet to be established as the investigation is still in progress. However, there is an argument – despite a widespread belief that the authorities haven't done enough to trace the assailants – that the same weapon was used in all three murders based on the report of the Kalina Forensic Science Laboratory (FSL) in Mumbai. However, since the Bengaluru-based FSL has asserted that different weapons were used in the murders of the three rationalists, the Central Bureau of Investigation (CBI) is considering the possibility of getting a third opinion and it told the Bombay High Court so in February 2016.[17]

The investigation into the killings of Dabholkar and Pansare in particular has placed the spotlight on the Sanatan Sanstha. Samir Gaikwad, who was arrested in September 2015 in connection with the murder of Pansare, is a sadhak of the Sanstha. Virendra Tawde, who was arrested in June 2016 in connection with the Dabholkar murder case, is also a sadhak. The charge sheet of the case, filed in November 2016, named Tawde as the prime conspirator and his fellow Sanstha sadhaks Sarang Akolkar, Vinay Pawar and Rudra Patril as the accused. In the Dabholkar case, the CBI, after interrogating several sadhaks, questioned the Sanstha chief Athavale and his closest aide Virendra Marathe at the Ramnathi ashram in February 2016. According to a report in *Mumbai Mirror* on 25 February 2016, 'A CBI team led by Additional Superintendent of Police S.R. Singh questioned Dr Athavale and one of the Sanstha's directors Virendra Marathe over two days in Goa at the organization's Ponda headquarters.'[18] Athavale was questioned for a second time in late February and early March in 2017, this time by the Special Investigation Team probing the murder of Pansare.

V

The revelation of the connection between the Sanstha and the murders might have shocked the world but the organization is flagrantly unapologetic. 'Our opposition to Dabholkar and Pansare is at the intellectual level,' Abhay Vartak, the spokesman of the Sanstha, said in an interview in October 2015. 'There is absolutely no violence and extremism in our ideology. We believe in elimination of the root cause rather than treating the symptoms.'[19]

Equally striking is the Sanstha's manic persistence in suing its critics for libel. A strong band of lawyers, organized under the Hindu Vidhidnya Parishad (HVP), appear to constitute a vital aspect of Athavale's 'spiritual' mission. 'These lawyers work very hard to protect sadhaks who are caught in various blast or murder cases and try to intimidate journalists and critics through a large number of defamation suits they have filed against them,' says Vijay Namdeo Rokade, whose Public Interest Litigation from 2011 seeking a ban on the Sanstha is still pending in the Bombay High Court.

Before they were murdered, Dabholkar and Pansare had to attend to a whole lot of defamation cases filed against them by the Sanstha. Eighteen defamation cases – both criminal and civil – had been registered against Dabholkar. 'Though none of the criminal cases against him led to a conviction, six civil suits were still pending in August 2013 when Dabholkar was killed,' says Rahul Thorat, who is also fighting a number of such cases. According to him, the Sanstha does not appear to be interested in pursuing these cases, it simply means to intimidate those who dare to write or speak against them. 'They have filed eleven cases against me for my writings. A few cases I have won, while others are pending. Sometimes they file a criminal case as well as a civil suit on the same issue.'

Though Athavale had earlier been surrounded by a band of lawyer disciples, the decision to organize them under the HVP was taken in 2012, when the Hindu Janajagruti Samiti – a Sanatan Sanstha outfit intended to eventually grow into an umbrella organization of all Hindu groups – held its first annual convention on the premises of the Ramnath Temple at Ramnathi. 'Providing legal service to the Guru is part of their sadhana,' says a lawyer who was once attached to the HVP. 'Every effort made in the courtroom by a Sanstha lawyer gets counted when his sadhana is measured by the Guru. There are plenty of them and so there is no need to outsource the Sanstha's legal requirements,' says the Mumbai-based lawyer while requesting anonymity for fear of reprisal.

An article published in the *Hindu* on 27 September 2015 examines how the Sanstha lawyers use defamation as a tool to harass critics and opponents.[20] The bulk of the litigation, according to the article, is in the courts of Mumbai and Panjim, though a good number have been filed in several other places in Maharashtra and Goa. Much of these are defamation cases against publications, journalists, editors and activists. The Sanstha's common tactic is to register a case outside the base of a publication or a reporter on the grounds that a particular article was read elsewhere. Asim Sarode, a Pune advocate who briefly represented journalists in a defamation case involving the Marathi magazine *Chitralekha*, describes the Sanstha members as employing intimidation tactics against defendants and their lawyers. 'The sadhaks gather outside court premises, they laugh at you, taunt you and even threaten you…I experienced this when I was appearing in the Goa court. I used to change my route while travelling to Goa, avoiding the Ponda mountain pass.' Sarode eventually had to write to the Maharashtra Home Department seeking protection.[21]

'[These are] the same tactics the Sanstha used in Ramnathi to silence villagers who were demanding, after the Madgaon blast in 2009, that its ashram be shifted from the village,' says Basant Bhatt, the priest who led the agitation. 'They filed three cases against me. All of them were meaningless. One of them is still pending in the court.'

The cases against Bhatt seem to have scared the villagers and dampened the agitation against the Sanstha. Sheker Naik, the former sarpanch of the Bandora Panchayat and another leader of the agitation, has also been bogged down with lawsuits. 'There was resentment against the ashram, but the fear of legal harassment made the villagers inactive for a while,' he says.

The murder of rationalists like Dabholkar, Pansare and Kalburgi once again brought the Sanstha into focus and revived the villagers' efforts to get rid of the ashram. The lead this time was taken by the Ramnath Yuvak Sangh, a local social outfit of village youth. In a press conference on 30 September 2015, a few days after the arrest of Samir Gaikwad in the Pansare murder case, the outfit's president, Saurabh Lotlikar, demanded that the Sanstha's ashram be removed from the village. 'People here do not want them in the locality because no one knows what they do,' he told mediapersons. Alleging that the Sanstha trained people to target others, he said: 'With all the news appearing, people are suspicious and do not want them to be here.'[22]

The Ramnath Yuvak Sangh also threatened to start a mass agitation if the government failed to shut down the ashram within seven days.[23] As this did not happen, the social outfit began a massive signature campaign in the village. Letters were also written on behalf of the villagers to the Governor of Goa, the state's chief minister, other members of the state cabinet and members of the state legislature.

'The Sanstha's success showed us how the system can be manipulated. It showed us how fascism comes into being,' says Lotlikar, admitting that the mass agitation that had almost rattled the ashram in 2009 could not be revived. 'Both the centre and the state are ruled by the BJP, and you can't expect this party to impose a ban on the Sanstha.' That may not be completely true. Even the previous Congress government at the centre, despite receiving a thousand-page dossier from the Maharashtra government in 2011 in the aftermath of a series of bomb blasts in 2008-09, kept mum on the topic of banning the Sanstha. Perhaps the Sanstha has well-wishers not just in the BJP but in other places too.

2
Hindu Yuva Vahini

I

On a bright February day in 1999 BJP Member of Parliament (MP) Yogi Adityanath swept out of the Muslim majority village of Panchrukhia in Maharajganj district of Uttar Pradesh with his armed followers. The heir to the position of Mahant at the Gorakhnath Temple was in his brand-new SUV, accompanied by a fleet of cars and bikes. The convoy then sped towards Maharajganj, an eastern Uttar Pradesh town adjacent to Gorakhpur, Adityanath's parliamentary constituency. But it was forced to a halt by Samajwadi Party (SP) workers who had gathered on the main road to court arrest under the leadership of Talat Aziz. They were demonstrating against the state's BJP government.

The confrontation quickly escalated from angry shouting to gunshots. Aziz's security guard, Head Constable Satyaprakash Yadav, received a bullet in his face and fell down, bleeding profusely. Scared, Aziz and her SP supporters fled into the fields on both sides of the road. Adityanath and his men, all members of the Goraksha Manch, drove leisurely away. Three hours later on 10 February 1999 the Maharajganj police filed an

FIR[1] against Adityanath and twenty-four others for a long list of crimes: attempt to murder (Section 307 of the Indian Penal Code), rioting (Section 147), carrying deadly weapons (Section 148), defiling a place of worship (Section 295), trespassing on a Muslim graveyard (Section 297), promoting enmity between two religious groups (Section 153A), and criminal intimidation (Section 506).

The FIR stated in detail how the Gorakhpur MP and his loyalists had tried to incite Hindus against Muslims in Panchrukhia and dug graves in the kabristan. It also stated that after the police started making arrests, they fled the village in fourteen or fifteen vehicles and resorted to firing at SP workers, injuring Satyaprakash Yadav (who later succumbed to his injuries) and three others.

The Panchrukhia incident took place a year after Adityanath joined active politics. He had become an MP from Gorakhpur in 1998, winning by a margin of 26,000 votes. In the 1999 polls, he defeated his SP rival Jamuna Prasad Nishad by a narrow margin of 7339 votes. He started the Goraksha Manch soon after his first victory but its efforts to polarize the electorate did not seem to have helped much in the 1999 elections.

The BJP fared miserably in the Uttar Pradesh state assembly elections in January–February 2002 and was dislodged from power by the SP. That Adityanath secured a victory for his aide Radha Mohan Das Agrawal – whom he fielded as an independent candidate after the

BJP denied him a ticket – did not offer any comfort for Agrawal's assembly seat accounted for barely one-fifth of Adityanath's parliamentary constituency.

It was this uncertain scenario that seemed to have inspired Adityanath to create a new organization that could provide him a broader base in his quest for electoral invincibility. The opportunity arose within a week of the declaration of the assembly election results.

On 27 February 2002, fifty-eight people died after a coach of the Sabarmati Express caught fire just outside the railway station at Godhra, a small town in Gujarat. The incident marked the beginning of one of the worst outbursts of violence against Muslims in recent Indian history. While Muslims in Gujarat were being subjected to terrible carnage, Adityanath was taking his first steps towards organizing a new anti-minority group in Gorakhpur.

The Goraksha Manch had little appeal beyond the followers of the Goraksha Peeth or the Gorakhnath Temple. A change of name was thus necessary to ensure that the organization could develop a wider base among Hindus. The Hindu Yuva Vahini (HYV), which subsumed the Goraksha Manch, was then set up with the intention of fulfilling Adityanath's electoral aspirations and making the appeal of its ideas grow beyond Gorakhpur.

Right from its inception, the HYV ran an aggressively toxic campaign of religious politics, turning even small incidents into full-blown communal wars and projecting minorities as the enemies of Hindus. It constantly sought to create a fear psychosis by emphasizing 'love jihad', the meat-eating 'habits' of Muslims, their 'propensity to violence', their 'deliberate disrespect' of Hindu rituals and national symbols, their 'tendency to dominate when in a majority' anywhere, etc.

The troubles sowed by the HYV in the region through its utterly communal acts and speeches eventually paid rich electoral dividends. Adityanath's victory margin in the Lok Sabha elections of 2004, for instance, rose to 1,42,000 votes from a meagre 7339 in 1999. The figure kept growing and crossed 3,00,000 in 2009 – a number that Adityanath managed to achieve once again in the 2014 Lok Sabha elections.

II

It is unusual for a sitting MP to form an organization outside the purview of his political party. But Adityanath knows the significance of maintaining an identity independent of the party he represents in the Lok Sabha. The separation that he maintains from the BJP and its patron the RSS is in accordance with a tradition that can be traced back to Digvijay Nath, the Mahant of the Gorakhnath Temple from 1935 to 1969, and one of the most politically astute sadhus of the twentieth century.

Born Nanhu Singh in 1894, a Thakur by caste, the orphaned Digvijay Nath was brought up in the

Gorakhnath Temple.² He joined the Hindu Mahasabha in 1939 and rose fast in the organization due to his status as the Mahant of the Goraksha Peeth and his political acumen. Like most Hindu Mahasabha members, he strongly opposed Mahatma Gandhi. On 27 January 1948 – three days before Gandhi's assassination – he had exhorted Hindu militants to kill him. Referring to his poisonous speech, the Commission of Inquiry into Conspiracy to Murder Mahatma Gandhi observed:

> V.G. Deshpande, Mahant Digvijay Nath and Professor Ram Singh [all Hindu Mahasabha leaders] at a meeting held on 27th [January 1948] at the Connaught Place under the auspices of the Delhi Provincial Hindu Sabha said that Mahatma Gandhi's attitude had strengthened the hands of Pakistanis... Mahant Digvijay Nath exhorted the gathering to turn out Mahatma Gandhi and other anti-Hindu elements.³

In 1949, as the party's president of the United Provinces, Digvijay Nath realized that the careful exploitation of the symbol of Ayodhya's Babri Masjid could give the Hindu Mahasabha a massive advantage over the Congress, particularly among the religious community it claimed to represent. He not only conceived the entire plot but also presided over the operation of surreptitiously installing the idol of Ram Lalla at the Babri Masjid in December 1949. While he held and pulled all the strings, the Mahasabha members in Ayodhya, working under the banner of the All India Ramayan Mahasabha, carried out the work on the ground.[4]

Soon after, Digvijay Nath was made the national general secretary of the Hindu Mahasabha. In an interview to the *Statesman* in June 1950, he declared that if the Mahasabha attained power, 'it would deprive the Muslims of the right to vote for five to ten years, the time that it would take for them to convince the government that their interests and sentiments are pro-Indian'.[5]

Digvijay Nath also worked closely with Swami Karpatriji, the founder of the Ram Rajya Parishad, another Hindutva party which like the Hindu Mahasabha had always distanced itself from the Sangh Parivar.[6] Despite his association with a different school of Hindutva thought, Digvijay Nath was always willing to look beyond his party and even collaborate – more in the form of patronage – with the RSS and its outfits to achieve his objectives. Thus, it was he who proved to be a facilitator when, after Independence, the RSS began to set up primary schools. Its first Saraswati Shishu Mandir was set up at Gorakhpur in 1952.[7] In 1966, when the VHP, an RSS body, set up the Sarvadaliya Gauraksha Maha-Abhiyan Samiti (Committee for the Great All-Party Campaign for the Protection of the Cow), Digvijay Nath was part of it.[8]

Yet he remained in the Hindu Mahasabha all his life and even became an MP on its ticket from Gorakhpur in 1967. He was the first Mahant in the tradition of the Gorakhnath Temple to actively participate in politics. It was under him that the temple underwent a radical transformation from a religious place venerated by Hindus and Muslims alike and one that mainly had a following of lower castes to a centre of religious and political power controlled by Thakurs.

Avaidyanath, who succeeded Digvijay Nath after the latter's death in 1969, also contested every election till 1989 on the Hindu Mahasabha ticket. However, in the late 1980s, when the Sangh Parivar took up the Ayodhya issue – the seeds of which had been planted by Digvijay Nath – a rapprochement took place between the two saffron traditions.

Within a few years, this reconciliation led to what is widely considered one of the most serious assaults on the Indian state, one that shook its very foundation. Avaidyanath played the pivotal role in this escalation in saffron politics. His speech at a meeting of sadhus organized by the VHP at the Allahabad Kumbha Mela of 1989, the Dharma Sansad, made the demolition of the Babri Masjid at Ayodhya imminent. A report on the Dharma Sansad said:

> Most of the clergy who spoke today [31 January 1989] took a strong anti-Muslim and anti-government tone. Mahant Avaidyanath of Gorakhpur pointed out that the Quran prohibited Muslims from constructing mosques

on the holy places of other religions. 'And telling us to construct the temple in another place to avoid conflict is like telling Lord Rama to wed another Sita to avoid war with Ravana.'[9]

Avaidyanath fought the Lok Sabha elections of 1991 and 1996 on the BJP ticket from Gorakhpur. Yet he retained a degree of autonomy which has been maintained by Adityanath, who succeeded him as the Mahant of the Gorakhnath Temple after the former's death on 12 September 2014.

III

Adityanath, like his predecessors Digvijay Nath and Avaidyanath, is a Thakur by caste. His real name is Ajay Mohan Bisht and he is a native of Yamkeshwar tehsil of Pauri district in Uttarakhand.[10] Avaidyanath, who also belonged to the same region, brought him to Gorakhpur, christened him Adityanath and declared him his heir in 1994. Four years later he made him his political successor too. In 1998, twenty-six-year-old Adityanath became the youngest MP in the Lok Sabha representing Gorakhpur. He has been re-elected four times since then.

Adityanath uses the BJP symbol every time he goes to the polls, and yet strives to retain complete hegemony within his fiefdom in eastern Uttar Pradesh through the HYV, independent of the RSS and any of its outfits. For this, he has employed the very methodology the RSS has practised over the past nine decades. Like the RSS, the HYV claims to be a cultural organization.[11] But political motivation is the sole factor that drives it.

On the ground, the members of the HYV act like a squad of goons who obey no one except Adityanath. He in turn seems to be well aware that his political fortune does not depend on the BJP or the RSS but is fuelled by communal polarization of an extreme kind. That, therefore, has remained the ideological raison d'être of the HYV since its inception. On paper, however, like any other organization, it has all kinds of office-bearers including presidents, vice presidents, secretaries, coordinators and members of the executive committees at the state, district, block and even panchayat levels.

Neither the leaders of the HYV nor its members ever address Adityanath by name or any simple respectful title. They refer to him with a string of honorifics – Goraksha Peethadhishwar Parampujya Yogi Adityanath Ji Maharaj, which they don't mind repeating more than once in a sentence. They even get upset if you ask them why all the laudatory titles are used even in normal conversation. (At least two leaders of the HYV, in fact, became so agitated after hearing this question that they almost threatened to leave the interview midway and calmed down only after much persuasion.)

'That only shows how much we all really love our leader,' explained Sunil Singh, the state president of the

HYV. Like every other member of the organization, he too had this bizarre habit. If nothing else, it is certainly one of the ways one can identify someone belonging to the HYV. There is another trademark as well – every HYV member flaunts a long saffron stole around his neck. 'That is one marker which separates us from others,' Singh pointed out.

Singh belongs to the Thakur caste and was one of Adityanath's most trusted lieutenants when he spoke to me in January 2016. He joined Adityanath's team in 1998 and held key positions at the HYV. According to him, 'In the beginning, there was a debate on the name. The first suggestion was to call the new organization Hindu Sena. Then Goraksha Peethadhishwar Parampujya Yogi Adityanath Ji Maharaj suggested it be called Hindu Vahini. Finally, it was decided that it would be Hindu Yuva Vahini.'

Once the name was finalized in March 2002, its members began organizing the youth of Gorakhpur city. 'The response was massive and within the first few weeks a large number of young men joined the Hindu Yuva Vahini in all sixty wards of the city,' recalled Singh, who was initially HYV coordinator in Gorakhpur district. 'It didn't take much time for Goraksha Peethadhishwar Parampujya Yogi Adityanath Ji Maharaj to realize that the Hindu Yuva Vahini must work with equal diligence in the neighbouring districts so as to make it more effective in Gorakhpur. Thus, on the day of Ramnavami that year, the Hindu Yuva Vahini was formally launched in a public meeting at Kushinagar.'

Adityanath then hand-picked all the office-bearers who would form the HYV's first Uttar Pradesh committee. Singh was elevated to the position of Uttar Pradesh president, while Raghvendra Singh, another Thakur and a close aide of Adityanath, was made the state coordinator. The two have held these positions ever since.

Adityanath also prepared a work schedule for HYV leaders to follow strictly through the year. From mid-January to mid-February, they were supposed to mingle with members of the Scheduled Castes and Scheduled Tribes by organizing a sahbhoj (common feast) in their localities. From mid-February to mid-March, they were to conduct a membership drive. Then, until the end of May, they had to organize public meetings and rallies. For the rest of the year, the HYV's state office-bearers visited different districts and concentrated on organizational work. In the beginning, the focus was on Gorakhpur; then it shifted to seven districts of Gorakhpur and Basti – Gorakhpur, Deoria, Kushinagar, Maharajganj, Basti, Sant Kabir Nagar and Siddharthanagar. The HYV's organizational work is now visible in many other districts of eastern Uttar Pradesh, including Faizabad, Gonda, Mau and Azamgarh.

Given the speed of its expansion, Adityanath has clearly done a good deal of careful organizational planning for the HYV. It has committees at several levels – state, district, block and panchayat. The work of a committee at the first three levels is considered complete as soon as its strength reaches 101. At the panchayat level, however, the full strength of a committee is achieved at 250, which necessitates the inclusion of a formidable number of young men in a village. 'When we meet the target, we put up a hoarding in the panchayat that carries the names of all the committee members,' said Sunil Singh. 'These members are also required to put up triangular saffron flags of the Hindu Yuva Vahini in their houses.'

According to Singh, organizational work in a district is considered complete only when all the panchayats in it, barring those with a negligible Hindu population or none at all, form their own committees. 'Until that happens, our teams tour specific villages every week to motivate the youth to join the Hindu Yuva Vahini. We have completed organizational work in Gorakhpur, Kushinagar, Maharajganj and Deoria. The work is in progress in other districts of eastern Uttar Pradesh.'

In 2005, the HYV started its own newspaper, a Hindi daily called *Hindavi*. With the support of Gorakhpur's local business community, Adityanath's outfit managed to run it for some time. But it had to be closed in 2007 because of 'financial and political problems'.[12]

The predominance of upper-caste Thakurs in most of the HYV's key positions is striking. Adityanath is a Thakur; so are Sunil Singh and Raghvendra Singh. This fact is evident not just at the level of the top leadership, it can even be seen in distant districts like Faizabad, where the HYV unit is headed by Rakesh Singh, a Thakur. It is also true in nearly all the districts of the Gorakhpur and Basti divisions where Adityanath's squad is most active.

'It sounds like caste-based discrimination but it goes further than that,' says Gorakhpur-based senior journalist Manoj Kumar.[13] 'How can the Hindu Yuva Vahini be different from its main source of strength, the Gorakhnath Temple, which is a Thakur Math since the days of Digvijay Nath? It was he who started the practice of appointing only Thakurs as the Mahants of this temple. Adityanath has only extended that practice to the outfit he runs.'

In addition, Adityanath also represents the legacy of Virendra Pratap Shahi, a Thakur gangster whose bloody caste-based rivalry against his brahmin counterpart Harishankar Tiwari has assumed mythical proportions in the districts of eastern Uttar Pradesh. The Thakur dominance in this region had suffered a setback in 1997 when Shahi was shot dead by an emerging brahmin gangster, Sri Prakash Shukla. Adityanath filled this particular void among the Thakurs, first with the Goraksha Manch and then with the HYV and even further by establishing the affluence of the Gorakhnath Temple and its reputation of being a Thakur Math.

This does not, however, stop the backward castes and dalits of the region from supporting Adityanath. In Manoj Kumar's opinion, 'The support of these castes is for the math and not for any individual Mahant. Dalits and backward classes have always been attached to the math despite the latter growing antagonistic and distant from the original concept it was founded upon. If Adityanath wants to test his personal strength, let him sever himself from the math and then contest the election.'

But doing this would require a particularly strong force of character. So far he hasn't given any indication that he is capable of such an action, notwithstanding the HYV's aggressive slogan at Gorakhpur, 'Gorakhpur mein rehna hai to "yogi, yogi" kehna hoga'. (To live in Gorakhpur, one has to chant 'yogi, yogi'.) Elsewhere in eastern Uttar Pradesh, the slogan runs, 'Poorvanchal mein rehna hai to "yogi, yogi" kehna hoga'. (To live in Poorvanchal, one has to chant 'yogi, yogi'.)

IV

It is notable that a man who takes pride in being seen as a brave Thakur don rather than a religious and political leader broke down famously on the floor of the Lok Sabha on 12 March 2007 after the local administration showed some spine in dealing with him and his outfit. The police crackdown was in response to the Hindu–Muslim riots that had erupted in and around Gorakhpur, caused in most part by the hate campaign orchestrated by Adityanath and the HYV.[14] Two people were killed and properties worth crores burnt, placing the region under curfew for several days during late January and early February in 2007.

This was by no means the first riot in which the HYV was clearly involved. In fact, communal riots became unusually frequent in Gorakhpur and its neighbourhood after the formation of the HYV in March 2002. It has either been involved directly or indirectly in virtually each of these incidents. What begins as a conflict between individuals from two communities turns into a communal flare-up only when Adityanath or other HYV leaders jump in.

There were at least six major riots in the region within the very first year of the HYV's formation. These incidents took place at Mohan Mundera village (Kushinagar district), Nathua village (Gorakhpur district) and Turkamanpur locality (Gorakhpur city) in June 2002; Narkataha village (Maharajganj district) in August 2002; and Bhedahi village (Maharajganj district) and Dhanghata locality (Sant Kabir Nagar district) in the first week of September that year. As the local administration remained ineffective, the communal disturbances continued unabated in the following years. Manoj Kumar, a local journalist who has chronicled such occurrences in the region, says, 'There have been at least twenty-two major riots in Gorakhpur and the neighbouring districts till Adityanath's arrest in 2007.'

Yogi Adityanath and over a dozen other leaders of the HYV were arrested while they were marching towards Gorakhpur's troubled areas on 28 January 2007, a day after he made an inflammatory speech aimed at turning a small commotion into a full-blown communal war. The arrest was timed such that the HYV could not carry out its threat of burning and destroying the tazia on 29 January. The tazia is a replica of Imam Husain's mausoleum at Iraq and it is the custom of Indian Muslims to bury the tazia on Muharram. Despite the arrests, sporadic riots broke out at various places in Gorakhpur and the neighbouring districts. In all, Adityanath had to remain in the lockup for eleven days; his bail was approved on 7 February.[15]

This was the first and only occasion when the local administration acted swiftly against Adityanath and his henchmen. The reason why the then chief minister of Uttar Pradesh, Mulayam Singh Yadav of the SP, chose to ease off on his policy of appeasement towards Adityanath – at least for a short while in January 2007 – remains a matter of debate. Perhaps he did so because Adityanath was instigating a major communal war just before the state assembly elections due in April–May that year. Locals argue that a battle along such lines would have weakened Mulayam even further in the polls by forcing Muslims to cast their votes in favour of his rival, Mayawati of the Bahujan Samaj Party.

Whatever be the reason, the arrest and the state government's decision to withdraw the security guards who had been assigned to protect Adityanath seemed to have unnerved him so much that his eyes welled up and tears rolled down his face as he explained to Lok

Sabha Speaker Somnath Chatterjee about what he called the 'political conspiracy' against him. A report in the *Hindu* said:

> The MP, who attended the House after spending 11 days in the Gorakhpur jail, wept while narrating his experience at the hands of the state government, alleging that it was out to 'malign and torment me'. A third-time member from Gorakhpur, he broke into sobs after Speaker Somnath Chatterjee allowed him to raise the issue during zero hour and promised to look into the matter. 'Will we get protection or will our condition be the same as that of Sunil Mahato?' he asked the Speaker. Mahato, a Jharkhand Mukti Morcha member from Jharkhand, was assassinated near Jamshedpur last week.[16]

The sight of Adityanath shedding tears shocked his Thakur supporters. It was seen as a sign of weakness unbecoming of a male belonging to a martial caste. Soon, however, his subordinates in the HYV started rebuilding his image, arguing that he was a sensitive man full of emotions even as many locals called him a coward capable only of spreading mob violence.

Nevertheless, as Adityanath's image of a firebrand leader took a serious hit, so did his outfit's activities in eastern Uttar Pradesh. For some time the HYV appeared to be in a shambles and Adityanath refrained from leading the mob and participating in attacks on Muslims as he was earlier wont to. Later, even as the HYV revived its organizational activities, his reactivation was restricted to making inflammatory speeches and participating in token actions.

In his speeches he still followed the same old extremist politics. But in action, he appeared to have become cautious even if he claimed to be the same old Yogi.

In essence, Adityanath and the HYV were now striving to keep the communal cauldron boiling – a strategy that became apparent during the run-up to the Lok Sabha elections in April–May 2014. Nearly two weeks after the murder of a Hindu trader on 4 December 2013 at Tanda in Ambedkar Nagar district, Adityanath intervened, but from a distance and with a vague threat. At a public meeting organized by the HYV on 16 December at Akbarpur, the district headquarters of Ambedkar Nagar, he put the blame on the SP's local MLA, Azim ul-Haq, and threatened to lead a march to Tanda if the arrest was not made within fifteen days.

The ultimatum period ended on 31 December 2013 but Adityanath was nowhere in sight to carry out his threat. On the ground, however, HYV activists kept the issue alive by starting a dharna at Tanda, and later, in the second week of February 2014, by organizing a demonstration outside the chief minister's residence at Lucknow. During the demonstration, two HYV

Hindu Yuva Vahini

activists even tried to immolate themselves but the police overpowered them easily.[17]

That Adityanath now wanted to act out only through his speeches was confirmed once again at a gathering of HYV activists on 29 December 2013 at Balrampur where he declared: 'Muslims consider terrorists their protector. Hindus must unite and remain alert wherever Muslims live and confront them if the situation so demands.'[18] Sunil Singh, his lieutenant, went a step further at the same meeting: 'In order to finish Islamic terrorism, Hindus must finish madrassas and mosques where training is given for terrorism... Shout "Jai Shri Ram" whenever you hear the Azaan... Workers of the Hindu Yuva Vahini will not allow Muslims to live in Hindustan.'[19]

V

With the exception of the arrest in 2007, police forces have by and large found it hard to deal with Adityanath and the HYV in Gorakhpur and its neighbouring areas. The political patronage that he enjoys and the rabble-rousing abilities of the HYV have resulted in the rule of law – so crucial for building confidence among the common people, especially religious minorities – being reduced to a fiction. Most cases involving Adityanath and HYV members have culminated in the transfer of local officials. This has bolstered Adityanath's image and sent the message that he and the outfit are above the law. The natural consequence has been the acute demoralization of local officials who have no option but to prostrate before the testosterone-fuelled unemployed young men running amok as cadres of the HYV.

It is not surprising that despite being named in a number of FIRs, Adityanath's name hardly ever figures in any charge sheet filed by the police after investigation. Even when Satyaprakash Yadav, the gunner deputed in the service of SP leader Talat Aziz, was shot in broad daylight at Panchrukhia village on 10 February 1999 and Adityanath's name appeared on top of the list of the accused in the police FIR, he and his followers remain scot-free till date. An inquiry by the Crime Branch–Crime Investigation Department (CB–CID), an investigation and intelligence wing of the state police, exonerated Adityanath in its report, claiming that the firing took place from both sides and it could not confirm where the bullet that led to the death of the head constable had come from.

Every time Adityanath or any HYV member figures in an FIR, a CB–CID inquiry comes to their rescue. This has remained a standard pattern in Gorakhpur. So far the local officials conducting CB–CID probes have not disappointed Yogi Adityanath.

Yet determined efforts have been made to bring back the rule of law in Gorakhpur. Talat Aziz appears determined, even seventeen years after the shooting

Hindu Yuva Vahini

incident, to push the case to its logical conclusion. 'Apart from the police FIR, I too filed an FIR,' says Aziz, who is now in the Congress. 'While the police has dropped its case against Adityanath following the CB–CID report, I have been pursuing it in the court. Despite all the manipulations of Adityanath, I am sure one day I will get justice and the court will direct the local administration to file a charge sheet against him.'[20]

Senior Urdu journalist Parvez Parwaz is another crusader whose determined legal battle to force the local administration to file a charge sheet against Adityanath for his inflammatory speeches and active role in the Gorakhpur communal riots of 2007 has turned him into a symbol of resistance. 'In the beginning I felt it would end in catastrophe. I had to sell whatever property I had so that I could pursue the court battle which seemed unending. But I had concrete evidence against Adityanath, and that sustained me even in the depths of despair,' he recounts.[21]

Parwaz's legal battle, which has been continuing for the past nine years, also indicates how the government apparatus at Gorakhpur is hell-bent on saving Adityanath. Despite having the recordings of his incendiary speech to HYV cadres on the evening of 27 January 2007, it took Parvez a tortuous journey of nearly two years through the court of the chief judicial magistrate of Gorakhpur and the Allahabad High Court to get the local police to file an FIR.[22]

'The police that was so reluctant to take cognizance of the case handed it over to the CB–CID within twenty-four hours after registering the FIR,' says Parwaz. 'I understood the game and moved the high court once again to seek a probe by an independent agency like the CBI. But before I could get any order, one of the accused obtained a stay from the Supreme Court against the earlier high court ruling through which the FIR had been registered.'

The Supreme Court upheld the high court order in 2012. 'After that began a prolonged CB–CID probe. Fearing foul play, I have filed a supplementary in the high court expressing my apprehension that the CB–CID might try to shield Adityanath since it has not recorded the statements of many of the witnesses. This is where the case stands now,' he says.

Parwaz is more than sixty years old now and is the victim of a chronic cough. Yet he roams the city fearlessly on his bike. 'I don't fear them. I have completed my life. But I will see to it that justice is delivered to the city before I die,' he says, laughing and coughing alternately.

VI

The swearing-in of Adityanath as the chief minister of Uttar Pradesh following the BJP's landslide victory in the state assembly elections in February–March 2017 may have been a dispiriting moment for most of the crusaders in Gorakhpur. But in no way does it mark the end of their efforts. Even at the height of his success, Adityanath finds on the table of the home department – the portfolio he has kept for himself – a request from the state police seeking sanction to prosecute him in the case pursued so earnestly by Parwaz.[23]

The request, in fact, has been pending since 2015, when the CB-CID, after completing its investigation into Adityanath's inflammatory speech and the riots that followed in 2007, sought the state government's permission to file a charge sheet against him and four others. Akhilesh Yadav, who was the chief minister till his party was routed in the 2017 elections, had pursued a policy of appeasement towards Adityanath and not taken any action on this request for two years. Now that Adityanath has become the chief minister, people are watching with interest whether he will allow himself to face trial. If he does, he might find it difficult to hold on to the post of chief minister. If he doesn't, he might face a much bigger uproar than what could be caused by Parwaz and others. Until this point, he had acted as the Mahant of the Gorakhnath Temple and got things done through his clout and influence. But now that he is the chief minister of Uttar Pradesh, it will be a great deal harder for him to evade media scrutiny of his actions, especially those pertaining to his own past activities.

Even the option of not taking any action in the manner of Akhilesh Yadav might not be feasible. The Allahabad

High Court, in an order passed on 10 March 2017, a few days before Adityanath's elevation to chief minister, asked the state government to apprise it of the status of the case. As this book goes to press, Adityanath and his government have kept mum on the issue.

Whatever be the outcome of the CB–CID's request, Adityanath's triumph could help him find a way to breathe life back into the HYV, which had split during the assembly elections when some members revolted because they were denied tickets by the BJP. The rebels, led by the HYV state president Sunil Singh, had even fielded candidates in over a dozen seats against the party for which Adityanath campaigned. Though none of the detractors won and some were sacked by Adityanath, there is no doubt that there had been a serious crisis in the HYV just months before he became the chief minister.

3
Bajrang Dal

I

The affable manner of forty-year-old Sharan Pampwell, the Mangalore-based leader of the Bajrang Dal in Karnataka, belies his exceptional business acumen. Like a good entrepreneur – obeying the laws of demand and supply – he has put to good use the anxiety felt by local businessmen as a direct result of the Bajrang Dal's activities. He offers them protection by using the foot soldiers of the very same Hindutva outfit he represents. The enterprise he has reared thus works both ways: the businessmen get security from the Bajrang Dal, and the Bajrang Dal activists benefit from regular employment in the establishments rendered vulnerable by their own acts of violence and hooliganism.

'We strictly follow the rules of business,' Sharan tells me as I sit down with him to understand the economics of his politics. 'Businessmen are prepared to work with us because we offer them security services at a very reasonable rate.'[1] Politics may once have been the sole reason for the existence of the Bajrang Dal – an aggressive youth brigade of the VHP, in turn an offshoot of the RSS – but in Mangalore, where this organization is very active today, it is a convincing profit motive that seems to drive its activities.

It works like this: first, the demand is created through the Bajrang Dal's agitational activities, which range from vigilantism to hooliganism to vandalism. This creates a sense of insecurity among owners of malls, shops and apartments. Then Eshwari Manpower Solutions Limited, a company owned by Sharan, offers security guards to the terrified businessmen so their fears are assuaged. The manpower for both these activities is drawn from the same pool. 'All the supervisors and the majority of the security guards who work for the company are Bajrang Dal karyakartas,' says Sharan. 'As the leader of the Bajrang Dal in this city, it is my duty to secure a livelihood for the karyakartas. But I don't turn away anyone who comes to me for a job. There is enough demand for security guards in the city. Some of our guards are even Muslims.'

Sharan Pampwell has had a meteoric rise in the Bajrang Dal since joining the organization in 2005. In 2011 he became the convener of the Mangalore division, and in 2014 was given the same designation in the south Karnataka region. In the Bajrang Dal's organizational structure, the state of Karnataka is divided into two units, north and south, each with its own convener. While in northern Karnataka the Bajrang Dal is weak, in the south it is hyperactive, perhaps far more than in any other part of the country.

With Eshwari Manpower Solutions Limited requiring constant business opportunities, the Bajrang Dal considers its agitational activities crucial to its economic gains under Sharan's leadership. 'I started this business soon after I was made the convener of the Mangalore division. Now I have the security contracts of three malls – City Centre, Forum Fiza and Big Bazar – apart from several shops and apartments in the city,' he said. City Centre at K.S. Rao Road and Forum Fiza at Pandeshwar are among the largest malls in Mangalore. Big Bazar, located in the Lal Bagh area of the city, is another important shopping complex.

Interestingly, most of the shops in City Centre and Forum Fiza belong to Muslims, the community that is the main target of the Bajrang Dal's attacks in Mangalore, as in other parts of the country. In Mangalore, however, the anti-Muslim basis of the Bajrang Dal's politics gives way to communal harmony the moment the Hindutva outfit doubles up as a business firm with minorities as clients.

Sharan tacitly admits this as he demonstrates his entrepreneurial shrewdness: 'We are getting a lot of business from Muslim shopkeepers and mall owners. That is primarily because they have faith in us and in our company.' He maintains silence about the secret of his success among minorities – the fear factor that compels Muslim businessmen to opt for Eshwari Manpower's security services. 'Given the kind of activities they [Bajrang Dal members] indulge in, this is the best way to do your business peacefully,' says a Muslim shop owner in City Centre.[2] 'In a city like Mangalore, if you don't outsource your security to them, you become extremely vulnerable. In the end, it is not a bad deal either. You do not just get security guards from them but also an assurance that you will be spared from any Hindutva activity. After all, one attack is enough to bring down your business.'

The transformation of the Bajrang Dal into a protection racket is not necessarily the natural progression of street-level Hindutva politics. It has been possible in Mangalore because of the widespread perception among businessmen and ordinary citizens that appealing to the police for protection is futile. When the state is unable to rein in troublemakers and the government's law and order machinery appears overwhelmed by them, perhaps the only option is to cooperate with the perpetrators of criminal culture.

II

The Bajrang Dal's approach to politics in Mangalore – small scale, local and business oriented – makes obvious sense for any organization which has as its main stock of activists unemployed youth from economically weaker sections of society. It is equally obvious why employment via the Bajrang Dal protection racket appeals to those who have struggled – and failed – to secure a livelihood in a highly competitive market.

However, when the Bajrang Dal was set up in 1984 by the VHP as its 'militant youth wing', its original objective was to increase Hindu mobilization for the Ayodhya movement, which the VHP had adopted as its central campaign barely a few months earlier. The epithet 'bajrang' (meaning strong and sturdy), which is associated with the name of Hanuman, the monkey god who led Lord Rama's armies into battle, was chosen to emphasize the muscle power of the members of this organization.

'Since the Bajrang Dal was dedicated solely to the construction of the Rama temple at the site of the Babri Masjid, Ayodhya's Vinay Katiyar [who had been an RSS pracharak since 1980] was chosen as its first national convener,' says Yugal Kishore Sharan Shastri, an Ayodhya-based sadhu who, as district convener of the VHP in Faizabad, was part of the deliberations that led to the formation of its youth wing.[3] In 1977, Shastri, a young sadhu residing in Ayodhya, became associated with the RSS and turned into a pracharak in 1981. Two years later, he was shifted to the VHP and made the head of its Faizabad district unit.

'Some weeks before the Bajrang Dal's formation, the VHP held a meeting at Kydganj in Allahabad. This meeting was attended by senior VHP leaders including Giriraj Kishore, Ashok Singhal, Thakur Gunjan Singh and Mahesh Narayan Singh as well as UP's district-level office-bearers of the VHP and the RSS. I was part of the VHP delegation representing Faizabad,' recounts Shastri.

'Before finalizing Katiyar's name, there was a discussion on the name of the new organization. Singhal suggested [it] be called the Bajrang Sena. Mahesh Narayan Singh, who was the VHP's organizing secretary in UP, differed, arguing that the term "sena" might not go down well with the government, which might consider it a troublemaker. He, therefore, proposed that the new body be called the Bajrang Dal, a name that was then adopted unanimously.'

Shastri did not survive in the VHP for long. In 1986, he snapped all ties with the Sangh Parivar as he felt that 'the VHP and the Bajrang Dal were not interested in the Rama temple per se, but only in diverting its political benefits to the BJP'. He has since been travelling extensively to different parts of the country, talking about the significance of communal harmony and attacking the politics of communalism. 'I was not alone in realizing this,' he says. 'Many sadhus of Ayodhya who had joined the VHP and the Bajrang Dal thinking that a temple for Lord Rama would be constructed fell inactive as soon as their real motive started becoming clear.'

That was perhaps the reason why the Bajrang Dal – despite its main objective being the construction of the Rama temple at Ayodhya and its national convener being a resident of Ayodhya – did not receive any significant response from local sadhus in the beginning. This was evident, as noted by Dutch anthropologist Peter van der Veer, by the indifferent way in which they greeted a VHP–Bajrang Dal procession arriving with much fanfare from Sitamarhi in Bihar with the mission of 'liberating the temple of Ayodhya'.

The procession – called the Ram–Janaki Rath Yatra – was the first big event organized to link the formation of the Bajrang Dal with the mobilization of Hindus for the Ramjanmabhoomi issue. It reached Ayodhya on the evening of 6 October 1984. A public meeting was organized the next day in its honour but local sadhus remained largely indifferent. Van der Veer writes: 'As far as I could see only some five to seven thousand people had come to listen to the speeches. This seemed a disappointing number... The Hindi press...inflated it to fifty thousand and in some papers even to a hundred thousand, numbers which were taken [up] by the national press.'[4] The next day, after halting at Ayodhya, the procession started for Lucknow to present a petition to the chief minister of Uttar Pradesh. 'Some of Ayodhya's sadhus had accompanied the procession to Lucknow,' according to Van der Veer, 'and told, after their return, that it had had a far greater success in Lucknow and in the places on the way than in Ayodhya itself.'[5]

Yet, despite the initial lack of enthusiasm in Ayodhya, the Bajrang Dal's popularity picked up fast in the rest of Uttar Pradesh and its neighbouring states as the general politics of the BJP, the VHP and the RSS started gaining momentum towards the end of the 1980s. The new organization had a central role in BJP leader L.K. Advani's Rath Yatra – a procession in a rath or chariot that began in September 1990 from the Somnath Temple in Gujarat and was scheduled to conclude in Ayodhya after winding some ten thousand kilometres through western and northern India. The Bajrang Dal's volunteers offered him a cup of their blood as proof of their commitment and kept him company.[6] They also often welcomed him by applying a tilak of blood on his forehead.[7] Activists also prepared the route of the yatra with decorations and the spread of communal propaganda.[8]

The Rath Yatra could not reach Ayodhya. Advani was arrested on the orders of Lalu Prasad Yadav's Janata Dal government in Bihar on 23 October. By then, however, it had succeeded in instilling so much confidence in the Bajrang Dal's activists that a week later, on 30 October, a group of them stormed the heavily guarded Babri Masjid in Ayodhya and placed a saffron flag on top of the structure. The resultant confrontation between the local police and thousands of kar sevaks led to several deaths.

After the BJP formed the government in Uttar Pradesh in 1991, it was the Bajrang Dal which directly participated in skirmishes on the Ayodhya issue while the prominent constituents of the Sangh Parivar – the RSS, the BJP and even the VHP – shunned any public posturing.[9] This was clearly a well-considered strategy where an affiliate organization lower down the hierarchy was deployed to keep an issue alive for future exploitation while the more important fronts remained relatively quiet to prevent any embarrassment for the BJP government.

Bajrang Dal

In 1992, just as it had done in 1990, the Bajrang Dal continued to act as the Sangh Parivar's main instrument for the mobilization of urban youth for kar seva. Its workers were at the forefront of the attack that led to the demolition of the Babri Masjid on 6 December 1992.

III

The demolition shook the nation but the P.V. Narasimha Rao government's approach to the development remained ambivalent. After four days, on 10 December 1992, it issued a notification banning the Bajrang Dal, along with the VHP and the RSS. However, it also adopted a conciliatory tone rather than a firm attitude towards the organizations – only a relatively small number of people were taken into custody and most of the key cadres were allowed to go into hiding. On 4 June 1993, a tribunal headed by a Delhi High Court judge, Justice P.K. Bahri, struck down the notification banning the Bajrang Dal and the RSS but upheld the ban on the VHP.

The Ayodhya agitation and the demolition of the Babri Masjid elevated the status of the Bajrang Dal among Hindutva forces. Its ranks swelled and its slogan – 'Jo Rama ke kaam na aaye, woh bekar javani hai' (A youth who cannot be put to the service of Lord Rama is worthless) – began to gain respectability in certain sections of society. On 16 December 1992, the RSS-linked Hindi daily *Swadesh*, published from Bhopal, carried an interview of Bajrang Dal activist Dharmendra Singh Gurjar in which he described in detail how his hundred-strong squad had undergone training and pulled down the Babri Masjid.[10] Other such disclosures began to appear in the press shortly thereafter.

It was in this context that the RSS set out to better control the Bajrang Dal, both structurally and ideologically, once the ban on it had been lifted. Until then, the outfit had operated with a loose structure and its members were recognized by their saffron headbands bearing the word 'Rama'. Now the process began to turn the Bajrang Dal into an all-India body with a more rigid structure that resembled the RSS in several respects. First, it was assigned a uniform – blue shorts, white shirt and saffron scarf. Second, trained RSS cadres were deputed to exercise control over the potentially violent organization. And third, large-scale training camps were organized for the Bajrang Dal's activists. In 1993, some 350 camps were held.[11]

In addition, a manual was prepared for those in charge of training the activists. In its preface, senior VHP leader Acharya Giriraj Kishore applauded the Bajrang Dal's role in the events of 6 December 1992: 'On that day the force of youth, escaping its leaders, and despite their repeated injunctions, went forward to accomplish its mission – a mission aimed to erase the shameful scar [that was the Babri Masjid].'[12] Kishore then elaborates on the need for discipline: 'Whether it is an individual or a nation, the entire society or an organization, only one who knows discipline can achieve success, awareness and excellence. Without discipline there can be no success. Discipline comes from training and exercise. And if a disciplined man is also brave, what more can you ask for?'[13]

The activists of the Bajrang Dal, however, have shown few signs of improvement when it comes to discipline. Unlike the RSS, it does not have regular shakhas. The training camps are organized from time to time but these are irregular and meant only to keep the volatile and semi-lumpen elements motivated. Lacking a regular ideological or physical training programme and a fixed schedule of activities – unlike the RSS – the Bajrang Dal seems to constitute a reserve force for the agitational activities of the Sangh Parivar.

Not that the organization hasn't expanded the scope of its actions. It is just that despite all the changes it has remained synonymous with force, coercion, aggression, rioting and even terror. In many ways, as Paul R. Brass points out, it resembles 'a fighting protection squad for the other organizations, a somewhat pathetic, but nevertheless dangerous version of the Nazi S.A.'[14] Moreover, the largely untrained status of the Bajrang Dal's workers in contrast to the thoroughly coached RSS cadres often absolves the larger front and the core organizations from direct responsibility for what the so-called responsible members of the Sangh Parivar term 'reckless acts of indiscipline and violence'.

Equally significant is the confusion that the Sangh Parivar seeks to create – perhaps deliberately – with regard to the background of the majority of the Bajrang Dal's adherents. Almost all the leaders of the RSS, the VHP and the Bajrang Dal I spoke to in course of my research asserted that the organization's cadres belong largely to the backward castes. This may not have been true in the beginning. Christophe Jaffrelot, in a study during the early and mid 1990s, finds an over-representation of the upper and intermediary castes from economically marginalized sections among the Bajrang Dal members who were part of the attack on the Babri Masjid.[15]

Jaffrelot explains the phenomenon in the context of the protests against the implementation of the Mandal Commission report, which recommended reservations in government jobs for backward castes, referred to in the Constitution as Other Backward Classes (OBCs). According to him, in August–September 1990, reacting to the V.P. Singh government's announcement that the Mandal Commission report would be implemented, many young men belonging to the upper and intermediary castes from humble economic backgrounds took to the streets. They feared that their career prospects would be reduced in the new quota regime, which would also affect the old social order.[16] 'In many cases, the same young people took part in both agitations [anti-Mandal as well as the Ayodhya agitations].'[17] The BJP was opposed to caste-based reservations and in August 1990 had favoured a quota system based on economic criteria. Advani's Rath Yatra, in fact, is said to have been planned in such a way as to defuse the OBCs' quota demands.

As it stands today, most Bajrang Dal activists are poorly educated young people who are either unemployed or who regard their jobs as unsatisfactory. Though the leadership belongs to the upper or intermediary castes, a substantial segment of the foot soldiers is drawn from the backward castes and even dalits. They are generally not interested in the doctrinal rigour or discipline that exists in the RSS shakhas and are keen to assert themselves by fighting those the Sangh Parivar prefers to treat as the 'other' – mainly Muslims and Christians. This does not, however, mean that simply acquiring a new identity makes lower-caste Bajrang Dal members always forget the socio-economic frustrations that drove them into the Hindutva fold. Caste-based discrimination makes the frustration erupt rather unusually sometimes. This can be seen, for instance, in the splitting of the Bajrang Dal's Mangalore unit which paved the way for the formation of the Sri Ram Sene. More on this in the next chapter.

IV

The VHP's official website calls the Bajrang Dal 'a security ring of Hindu society'.[18] However, the outfit's activities have proven just the opposite. With its anarchic structure and disposition, it is a rogue child of the Sangh Parivar.

In 1999, barely fifteen years since its formation, a group of activists led by the Bajrang Dal's Rabindra Kumar Pal alias Dara Singh burnt alive Australian missionary Graham Staines and his children. Staines had been working with leprosy patients in Odisha for thirty years before he was murdered that cold January night. While he and his two little sons slept in his car at Manoharpur village in Keonjhar district, a mob poured petrol over it and set it afire. The Staines tried to escape but the mob prevented them and all three were charred to death.

Soon it came to light that the incident was the handiwork of men belonging to the Bajrang Dal. Odisha's director general of police B.B. Panda put an official stamp on this finding, saying: 'The Bajrang Dal was behind the attack.'[19] Investigations revealed that it was the local leader Dara Singh who led the mob on the night of 2 January 1999. In 2003, a trial court awarded him the death sentence, which was commuted to a life term by the Orissa High Court in 2005. In 2011, the Supreme Court upheld the high court order.

The Bajrang Dal, perhaps emboldened by the fact that the BJP, another Sangh outfit, was in power at the centre, continued to display its appetite for bloodletting. Its activists attacked churches, priests and nuns in several parts of the country. Most shocking of all, however, were its activities in Gujarat, where it was – and is even today – probably in its most organized form. The outfit was heavily involved in the incidents of communal violence

Bajrang Dal

against Muslims that engulfed large parts of the state in 2002. Together with the VHP, the Bajrang Dal was identified as the most active of the instigators responsible for the organization of mobs in Gujarat's urban and rural areas.[20]

Bajrang Dal activist Babu Bajrangi has gone on record to boast about his actions.[21] He admitted that he armed a mob of locals in a nearby area and attacked Naroda Patiya on 28 February 2002. They killed as many Muslims as they could find and burned Muslim shops, going by a list they had obtained from the VHP.[22] Referring to the burning of Muslims, he was taped saying: 'We believe in setting them on fire because these bastards say they don't want to be cremated, they are afraid of it, they say this and that will happen to them…'[23]

If in 2002 the Bajrang Dal provided men and organized killer mobs, in later years it actively carried out the Sangh Parivar's agenda of the separation of communities. In Gujarat, it went on a crusade to 'rescue' Hindu girls who had married Muslims or men from a different caste. One of its pamphlets in 2007 explained that love marriages harmed Hindu tradition and that rescuing a Hindu girl was equivalent to saving a hundred cows.[24]

The activities of the Bajrang Dal and other Sangh outfits vitiated the atmosphere so much that in most cities Muslims started increasingly to seek safety in numbers, leading to large-scale ghettoization in the state. In fact, most cities in Gujarat now have some large Muslim pockets which are referred to locally as 'mini Pakistan'— a term connoting that everyone living there is an 'enemy'. These pockets are often separated by walls which keep getting higher with every riot. Even in elite areas Muslims are not allowed to buy property. According to a 2004 report in *Frontline*, 'When Muslims bought flats in Paldi, an upmarket area of Ahmedabad, Bajrang Dal activists ransacked the building and threw a bomb that blasted the lift. Later, they forced the Muslim owners to sell their flats at a pittance. In Ahmedabad's walled city, the Bajrang Dal attacked traders who sold property to Muslims.'[25]

After the communal violence of 2002 the ghettoization of Muslims began happening even in parts of rural Gujarat. 'Many refugees have been unable to return to their homes. They prefer to stay in nearby towns or villages with a relatively large Muslim population. They feel that isolation makes them easier targets. After hounding out Muslim residents of villages, local Bajrang Dal units proudly put up banners proclaiming them to be "Muslim Free".'[26]

More sinister was the evidence that began to pour in about the Bajrang Dal changing its methods of operation from group violence to covert brutality patterned on international terror groups. This was first noticed in April 2006 at Nanded in Maharashtra where two of the organization's activists died while making explosives at the residence of RSS worker Laxman Rajkondwar. Similar blasts were reported from other towns in Maharashtra like

Parbhani, Jalna and Purna, and investigations indicated that these were no ordinary crimes. They pointed to the possibility of a larger Bajrang Dal conspiracy wherein members disguised as part of the minority community assembled bombs to target mosques, thus camouflaging their entire operation to resemble a terror operation run by Muslims. Further delving revealed that around three dozen Bajrang Dal activists from all over Maharashtra were trained in Pune, while another hundred members from around the country were trained in Nagpur. It was also disclosed that the men who trained the cadres of the Bajrang Dal included retired officers of the military and intelligence services.[27]

Two years later a similar incident was reported from Kanpur where two Bajrang Dal activists, Rajiv Mishra and Bhupinder Singh, died while making explosive devices on 24 August 2008. The inspector general of police (Kanpur zone) told journalists that investigations by Uttar Pradesh's Special Task Force had revealed 'plans for a massive explosion'. The police recovered 3 kilograms lead oxide, 500 grams red lead, 1 kilogram potassium nitrate, 11 countrymade grenades, several bomb pins, seven timers and batteries from the scene of the blast. The countrymade hand grenades were similar in shape and size to those used by the defence forces. In raids related to this incident, the police found a diary and a hand-drawn map of Muslim-dominated Firozabad, Uttar Pradesh. The map had markings of at least five spots which might have been possible targets.[28] According to Kanpur Senior Superintendent of Police Ashok Kumar Singh, 'Though test reports from FSL, Agra, will take some time, we know that the explosives stored in the room were enough to cause damage. Mishra and Singh had held significant posts in Bajrang Dal in the past, and the investigation so far clearly indicates their objective.'[29] The deputy inspector general of the Uttar Pradesh Anti-Terrorism Squad said: 'Their intention was to plant bombs. The probe will further decipher the motive.'[30]

In 2008, when anti-Christian riots broke out in Kandhamal in Odisha, the Bajrang Dal was once again in the eye of the storm. There were allegations of its involvement in the communal violence that followed the killing of the VHP's Swamy Lakshamananda Saraswati and four of his supporters, allegedly by Maoist rebels. The violence started immediately after the VHP leader's murder. The official death toll was thirty-eight but unofficial estimates pegged the casualties at ninety-three. In addition, there were widespread attacks on Christian tribals and churches that resulted in the displacement of over 50,000 people.

The role of the Bajrang Dal in the blasts and the Kandhamal riots led different quarters to demand a ban on the body. National Security Advisor M.K. Narayanan, however, opposed the idea, saying a ban might not be sustainable. He proposed that an increased number of Bajrang Dal activists be arrested 'based on the information we have... You can ban it but you will not be able to sustain it'.³¹ He argued that an organization could not be banned without adequate preparation and that it should instead be dealt with effectively 'because then there are many copycat organizations...several micro units of the same kind may come up'.³²

V

Narayanan perhaps had a point. Being largely a collection of inchoate street gangs, the Bajrang Dal could not have been tamed simply by a ban. To deal with it effectively would have required a much more comprehensive and determined approach than any government has ever shown in the past. In any case, rioting and terror activities have not been the only specializations of the Bajrang Dal. All through it has also been implementing a form of cultural policing directed against artists, writers and anyone who appears to deviate from its definition of Hindu culture and tradition.

In the beginning, its primary targets were artists who did not fit in with this definition. In 1996, M.F. Husain was attacked for his 1976 painting which depicted a scantily clad goddess Saraswati. Thereafter, the attacks became frequent. For years Husain waited for legal protection, and when it did not come he ended up having to leave his home country.

The Bajrang Dal has also targeted Hindu artists for

their 'immoral' depiction of Hindu deities. In January 2004 on its direction a group vandalized the Garden Art Gallery in Surat, destroying several canvasses not only by Husain but also by painters like K.H. Ara, N.S. Bendre and Chittrovanu Mazumdar. Again, in May 2007, its target was the fine arts department of MS University, Vadodara, where a student was accused of painting obscene pictures using religious themes.[33]

They have also launched campaigns against plays and films that did not conform to their idea of Hindu culture. In 2004, *Ponga Pandit*, a play that denounced the condition of dalits, faced the wrath of the Bajrang Dal, which also agitated against the portrayal of widows in Deepa Mehta's film *Water* and ransacked the sets. Her earlier film, *Fire*, which told the story of a lesbian relationship, had also infuriated the Bajrang Dal.

Valentine's Day celebrations have been an easy point of attack for organizations like the Bajrang Dal. The sight of young men and women freely roaming in parks and exchanging roses, chocolates and other gifts have irked its activists so much that every year they come out in large numbers to spoil the celebrations. They harass young couples by blackening their faces, forcing them to perform marriage rituals or tie rakhis, sometimes even thrashing them.

The formation of the BJP government at the centre in May 2014 seems to have given the Bajrang Dal a fresh shot in the arm as it once again started capturing news headlines for violence. Now it appears to be focused primarily on religious conversion and the enforcement of a ban on the consumption of beef. In December 2014, merely months after Narendra Modi came to power, the Bajrang Dal made news for organizing the 'voluntary' conversion of nearly three hundred Muslims to Hinduism at Agra in Uttar Pradesh. Soon, however, the truth came out. Most of the Muslims who followed its diktat were miserably poor and living in a slum on the outskirts of Agra. They were migrants from Bangladesh and didn't even have ration cards. Some of them told the media that they were misled to convert by a Bajrang Dal programme which they thought was for registering them as Below Poverty Line (BPL) families – a status that entails some basic survival support from the government. Others claimed that they changed their religion out of fear of violence from Hindutva groups.[34]

Such forced conversions – which the Bajrang Dal and other Hindutva forces call 'ghar vapasi' or reconversion to Hinduism – became frequent, emboldened by Modi's silence. On 29 January 2016, a man named Awadhesh Kumar was tonsured, garlanded with shoes and paraded on a donkey by Bajrang Dal activists in Jalaun district of Uttar Pradesh. According to the police, the Bajrang Dal believed that Kumar was instrumental in getting four Hindus converted to Christianity. The police later filed an FIR against '100–150 unidentified Bajrang Dal men' and made a few arrests.[35] Usually, this is where such a case ends. That the Bajrang Dal would get away with it this time too became clear when the police also registered a case against Awadhesh Kumar for promoting enmity between different groups on religious grounds.

Demanding a complete ban on beef – an old RSS agenda – has been another pretext used by the Bajrang Dal to unleash violence after Modi became the prime minister. In September 2015, for instance, it held a demonstration at Jammu demanding capital punishment for those slaughtering bovine animals and participating in the sale or purchase of beef in Jammu and Kashmir.[36]

When Mohammad Akhlaq was beaten to death on 28 September 2015 in Dadri, Uttar Pradesh, by a Hindu mob riled by rumours that he and his family had slaughtered a cow and were eating beef, the Bajrang Dal stood not by the victim but by the murderers. Without delay, it offered legal assistance for the perpetrators of the crime. Bajrang Dal spokesman Balraj Dungar also warned that Uttar Pradesh could see 'another 1857' if a complete ban on beef was not imposed. 'Why did the revolt of 1857 take place? People rose because the British Raj did not respect religious and cultural sensibilities. If the UP government lets cow slaughter go on, the people will rise again.'[37]

The Bajrang Dal has steadfastly continued its campaign of harassment. On 15 March 2016, the police arrested four Kashmiri Muslim students at Mewar University in Chittorgarh, Rajasthan, after its activists alleged they were cooking beef in a hostel room. Later, when it was found to be mutton and not beef and when their arrest started making national headlines, the police told the media that they had picked up the Kashmiri students to save them from the Bajrang Dal.[38]

So far we've seen that the Bajrang Dal has had its hands in everything from riots to blasts to vigilantism. That they can double up as 'entrepreneurs' rather seamlessly in Mangalore without the need for a massive image makeover might well be due to Sharan Pampwell's ability to exploit both the heightened sense of insecurity among Muslim businessmen and the fallen credibility of the police to provide safety against the Bajrang Dal's activities. However, in the absence of adequate employment opportunities, it is not surprising that a large number of youth find the anarchic capitalism of Hindutva appealing.

4

Sri Ram Sene

I

An anonymous call in the third week of November 2015 almost prompted Pramod Muthalik, the president of the Sri Ram Sene, to go underground. The caller did not reveal his identity but Muthalik suspects he belonged to a Muslim terror outfit. 'In a heavy voice, he told me that I should start counting my days and that his men would shoot me wherever I am spotted.'[1] Muthalik had received threats in the past but they had been indirect. It was different this time. This call had been made directly to him and he was taking it seriously because 'Muslim terrorists are always two steps ahead of everyone in the game'. As a precaution, he stopped meeting strangers, agreeing to a rare request only after getting the person's details thoroughly verified. He became discreet in his movements around town, ensuring he was always surrounded by several circles of his trusted supporters. 'I have no choice,' he said. 'They'd kill me. You don't know them. There must be a lot of them on the lookout for me.'

That was Muthalik when I met him in Hubli, Karnataka, during the last week of November 2015. The

Sene chief was the most recognized face of Hindutva in Karnataka. His presence on TV jacked up TRPs so much that he was always in great demand for prime-time shows. But he seemed to have become a paler version of himself after the harsh reality check. The phone call might well have been a hoax but the way it affected him showed that all was not well. Perhaps the world he had thrived in had changed. That also explained why he was not able to trust the security cover provided by the government. There were, in fact, two policemen guarding him all the time. He also got escorts whenever he went out of the city. But he considered it all quite inadequate. 'Believe me,' he said, 'this security wouldn't be able to stop them. No, I can't take the risk.'

The beginning of Muthalik's downward spiral can be traced to the very same moment when he seemingly reached the pinnacle of success. In March 2014, when the BJP's prime ministerial candidate Narendra Modi was making waves, Muthalik, by virtue of his firebrand image created by the controversial activities of the Sri Ram Sene, had become the Hindutva icon of Karnataka. In a formal ceremony on 24 March he joined the BJP with much fanfare, vowing 'to ensure Modi becomes PM', in the presence of the Karnataka BJP president Prahlad Joshi, former chief minister Jagdish Shettar and former deputy chief minister K.S. Eshwarappa.[2] Within hours, however, the central leadership of the BJP forced the state unit of the party to cancel Muthalik's membership.[3] 'It all took five hours,' recounted the Sene chief. 'At 11 a.m. I was inducted into the party and at 4 p.m. my membership was cancelled.'

At our meeting, Muthalik claimed he was neither surprised nor worried by the episode but it was pretty obvious that even after one and a half years the issue still weighed heavily on his mind. 'I knew what was happening,' he said. 'I was a potential threat to some of the top BJP leaders from Karnataka. They would have never allowed me to remain in the party.' The implication, too, was clear to him. 'The doors had been shut on me by the party which had benefited from my work in Karnataka so much.'

Muthalik, however, persisted and filed his nomination papers from two Lok Sabha constituencies in Karnataka: Dharwad and Bengaluru. 'Dharwad because I have my base there and Bengaluru city because it was the constituency from which [BJP leader] Anantha Kumar was contesting,' he explained. 'I wanted to give Anantha Kumar a fight because it was he who ensured my expulsion from the BJP.' The Sene chief lost in both constituencies but he put up a brave face. 'At least I was able to send the BJP a message – that it cannot use Karnataka as a springboard from where it can spread to other parts of South India without my cooperation.'

Clearly, the expulsion from the BJP was both a blow and an insult that Muthalik has not been able to forget. It took away the protective political shield he had enjoyed until then, leaving him quite vulnerable. 'I used to ignore anonymous threats and telephone calls earlier. In 2009, for example, I received serious threats to my life but I wasn't bothered by them,' he said. 'Now the situation has changed. I know that no one in the BJP would be allowed to stand up for me because I'd pose a threat to some of the party leaders if I survive. The Congress, anyway, is an enemy party for us.'

Though rifts like this take a long time to heal, in November 2015 Muthalik seemed keen, almost desperate, to mend fences with the BJP. Though he had serious problems with 'a section of BJP leaders, particularly Anantha Kumar', he still called himself 'a fan' of Narendra Modi. He was certain it wasn't Modi's idea to throw him out of the BJP. 'Like me, he is also facing conspiratorial moves by some of the BJP leaders. I can clearly see that some BJP leaders are jealous of Modi.' As for his future prospects with the party, he appeared hopeful but stopped short of talking about it.

II

Muthalik has been able to exercise greater control over what is known about him than almost any other Karnataka politician because he spent his childhood and youth being schooled in RSS ideology. He hasn't won an election and has thus avoided any minute scrutiny that would have made it difficult for him to conceal personal information. We know about him either through his claims about himself or what the courts have revealed about him.

Unsurprisingly, he has been a frequent occupant of a jail cell. 'The first time I went to jail was in 1975 when Indira Gandhi imposed Emergency. I was arrested because I was working as an underground member of the RSS.' He was around twenty years old at that time and had just completed his graduation. 'I was detained in Belgaum Jail for about a month and I came out of it as a full-time pracharak of the RSS.' After that, being in prison became a regular affair for him. By the end of 2015, when we met, he had lost count of the number of times he had been arrested.

Muthalik said his real journey began only after he was thrown behind bars. 'It was in Belgaum Jail that I got the opportunity to interact with some of the senior RSS leaders in Karnataka. The ideology was not new to me. My father used to attend the RSS shakha regularly and so I grew up in that very background. But the discussions I had with RSS leaders in jail shaped my relationship with Hindutva so much that I decided to work for this ideology for the whole of my life.'

Muthalik seemed reluctant to discuss all that he did 'for the sake of Hindutva' during the next seventeen years. His only observation was: 'I travelled on the path I found in jail, working as a pracharak and carrying out the responsibilities given to me by the RSS at different places in the country.' In 1993 he was shifted to the RSS's rather flamboyant cultural outfit, the VHP. But his real journey – the one he had 'longed for' – began in 1994. 'On one fine morning that year, [the VHP leader] Ashok Singhal called me and asked me to organize the Bajrang Dal's unit in Karnataka,' he said. 'Working as the head of an organization in my state was something I had always wanted to do. I, therefore, immediately accepted Singhal's proposal. I was made the convener of the Bajrang Dal in Karnataka.'

Within a few years, the Bajrang Dal spread its roots in the state, particularly in its northern and coastal regions. 'In 1997, we organized a Bajrang Dal conference which was attended by over 3000 members,' Muthalik said. 'In 2001, I was made the Bajrang Dal's convener for the four south Indian states of Karnataka, Andhra Pradesh, Tamil Nadu and Kerala.' Partly because of the activities of the Bajrang Dal, the BJP registered an impressive performance in the Karnataka assembly elections of 2004 – it got seventy-nine seats in 224 constituencies, marking a huge improvement over forty-four seats in the 1999 polls and forty in 1994. 'More than half the MLAs who won in 2004 had come from a Bajrang Dal background. The RSS too benefited from our activities. Its shakhas rapidly spread in villages during those years.'

The enhancement of Muthalik's status in the Sangh Parivar following the results of the 2004 polls proved to be short-lived. 'That was the first time I was seen by many in the Karnataka BJP as a threat,' he claimed. Before long his newfound glory led to his isolation in the Parivar. 'Rumours began to circulate that I was of loose character and that I was using the organization to make money. I met the top leaders of the Sangh and tried to clear the air but by then they had got carried away by rumours,' he said.

Muthalik left the Bajrang Dal in 2005 to try his luck at other organizations. The first to grab his attention was the Shiv Sena. He held meetings with Bal Thackeray, the Shiv Sena chief, and set out to organize the party's units in Karnataka. 'At first it was a relief for me. In some ways life was better there. My ideology matched with that of the Shiv Sena and Bal Thackeray gave me a free hand in Karnataka,' he said.

Belgaum, where Muthalik lived, has a strong Marathi population, and forming the Shiv Sena's units there may not have posed a big challenge. Within months, Muthalik started getting a good response from locals and Shiv Sena units soon started opening up in other parts of the state. 'And then, even before the Shiv Sena could get a proper foothold in Karnataka, I suddenly realized that it could not go any further,' he said. 'There erupted a tussle between Marathi and Kannada language fanatics. Belgaum, which was claimed by Maharashtra as part of its cultural zone, became the centre of this debate. Kannada language groups started disrupting the Shiv

Sena's meetings, and working for that party in Karnataka just became impossible.'

Muthalik suspected that all this was orchestrated by the Sangh Parivar, which didn't want to let a second Hindutva party develop roots in Karnataka. In 2006, the Shiv Sena's fate in Karnataka was sealed, and Muthalik left the party with all his friends and associates. 'It was a big shock. I again started thinking about how to remain relevant.' The same year he formed a political party, the Rashtriya Hindu Sena, and close on its heels, registered the Sri Ram Sene as a trust.

III

Interestingly, the Sri Ram Sene was not Muthalik's idea. The idea first took shape among his lieutenants in Mangalore who had left the Bajrang Dal in 2005 along with him but were fuelled by different factors. While Muthalik's was a highly personalized fight within the Sangh Parivar, his henchmen in Karnataka were filled with indignation at the brahminical dominance of the RSS and the BJP.

Coming mostly from the backward castes, these Mangalore-based leaders – Praveen Walke, Arun Kumar Puttila, Prasad Attavar, Anand Shetty, Subhash Padil and others – had played a central role in making coastal Karnataka a saffron bastion. 'Till 2004 we didn't feel any brazen discrimination on caste lines,' says Walke, who at that time was the Bajrang Dal's state convener.⁴ 'But once the assembly election results that year showed the task was complete, caste became our handicap in the organization which keeps all its important positions reserved for brahmins. Nobody in the Sangh will tell you this, but everything there works to benefit brahmins. Lower-caste people have to do the lower-level work – you could say the dirty work – of fighting on the streets.'

Walke started his journey in the Bajrang Dal at almost the same time as Muthalik. After taking charge of the Bajrang Dal in Karnataka in 1994, the first thing Muthalik did was make Walke the convener at Mangalore. 'That year there was a meeting at Hampi where the responsibilities were distributed for organizing the Bajrang Dal in Karnataka. I got the responsibility of Mangalore,' says Walke, a vaishya by caste. In a short time, Walke built a network of local leaders and grassroots activists in Mangalore and nearby areas and gradually turned Dakshina Kannada, an erstwhile Congress base, into the saffron stronghold of Karnataka.

'As we started gaining strength, we also began to realize we were not getting our due because of our backward caste origin,' says Walke. 'We were dismayed by this attitude of the brahmin leaders of the RSS. So once Muthalik told me sometime in 2005 that he had left the Sangh, we all came out of the Bajrang Dal and joined him.' For a brief while, Walke and his associates joined the Shiv Sena and then left it along with Muthalik. When Muthalik formed the Rashtriya Hindu Sena, they joined that too, but reluctantly because they didn't want to be part of a political party.

'It was then that one day in 2006 all of us in Mangalore held a day-long meeting at my place and decided to form an organization similar to the Bajrang Dal,' recounts Walke. 'Arun Puttila suggested the name Sri Ram Sene. We all agreed.' Besides Walke and Puttila, the meeting in Dongarkeri, Mangalore, was also attended by other former Bajrang Dal activists from the region like Mohan Bhatt, Subhash Padil, Prasad Attavar and Anand Shetty. 'We then informed Muthalik of our decision to form the Sri Ram Sene and invited him to lead this organization. He agreed, came here and with our consent got the organization registered.'

Soon the Sene became hyperactive in and around Mangalore, getting involved in most of the cases related to communal tension, vandalism and moral policing. For a while, it seemed as if the Bajrang Dal, which had already lost a substantial chunk of its local leaders and cadres, had foregone much of its agitational space to the Sene. The rule of law became something of a fiction in the city. Indiscriminate looting and atrocities against minorities were the order of the day. For the sake of its survival the Bajrang Dal, too, revived its activities. Caught in the throes of two competing syndicate-like Hindutva organizations, communal riots took place in Mangalore and its neighbouring areas with unusual frequency and ferocity during 2006.

'We had rich experience as leaders of agitation, and our boys were rearing all the time for street-level showdowns,' recalls Walke. 'The media started covering us as if we were the sole organization in the region, and we began issuing statements to the press like you order coffee. It seemed for a while that the Bajrang Dal had simply vanished. We had forty-two cases against us within two months of the formation of the Sene.'

The early success also gave rise to a clash of ambitions within the Sri Ram Sene. In the beginning it ran its show without declaring the full structure of its organization. While Muthalik was called its national president, Walke was named the state convener. 'Around the beginning of 2007, we called a meeting and invited Muthalik to preside over it. In that meeting, he was to announce the names and responsibilities of all the office-bearers of the Sri Ram Sene,' says Walke. 'Just before the announcement could be made, one of our senior leaders, Prasad Attavar, inserted his name in the list of office-bearers as the co-convener of Karnataka. I didn't know of this because I was occupied with the management of the meeting and had no inkling that there might be some last-minute changes. I brought up the issue with Muthalik but he refrained from intervening directly and went on to announce the amended list of office-bearers.'

For Walke and many of his associates, including

Anand Shetty, this was a clear betrayal. 'My argument was simple – two state conveners would lead to internal bickering and factionalism which would weaken the organization,' he says. 'Since Muthalik and Attavar were not ready to correct the mistake, arguing that the list of office-bearers had already been made public, I decided to withdraw from the organization.'

Thus, within months of the establishment of the Sri Ram Sene, Walke, one of its central figures in Mangalore, chose to stage an exit. 'Some local leaders and cadres also left the organization along with me. At that time I ran an interior decoration company, and nearly seventy people worked for it. I began to concentrate on my business and stopped participating in the Sene's meetings and activities.'

The weakening of the Sene leadership at Mangalore emboldened its rival, the Bajrang Dal, and spurred it to make a fresh bid to recapture lost ground. And it did indeed succeed to an extent but the initial momentum of the Sene remained largely unaffected.

IV

Yet, the Sri Ram Sene remained active, with its leaders constantly trying to strengthen the organization's 'Hindu' identity. In Delhi, it first made news on 24 August 2008, when a few Sene members barged into an art exhibition organized by SAHMAT, a non-governmental

Sri Ram Sene

organization, and destroyed several M.F. Husain paintings. They also left behind a handful of pamphlets denouncing Husain.

In September of the same year, Muthalik declared that 700 members of the Sri Ram Sene were being trained to carry out suicide attacks. His announcement came in the aftermath of the Bengaluru bomb blasts. 'We have no more patience. Tit for tat is the only mantra left to save Hinduism,' the Sene chief declared at a public event in Mangalore. 'If centres of religious importance for Hindus are targeted, twice the number of religious centres of the opposite party will be smashed. If Hindu girls are exploited by members of other religions, double the number of girls from other religions will be targeted.'[5] In January 2009, the Karnataka police arrested nine people in connection with the Hubli bomb blasts during the 2008 state assembly elections. The mastermind, Nagraj Jambagi, was a Sene member and a close associate of Muthalik.

Even so, the Sri Ram Sene could never have captured headlines in the national and international media if its members had not barged into Mangalore pub Amnesia on 24 January 2009 and beaten up a group of young women because they were violating 'Hindu culture and tradition' by drinking publicly. The video of the incident remains one of the most watched clips on YouTube. It is a mystery as to how a TV crew happened to be there, ready to shoot the 'unannounced' attack at the pub. The recording sparked nationwide outrage two days later on Republic Day when television channels broadcast footage of women being slapped, beaten and chased out of the pub by Sene men. It stirred up such intense debate that even news producers from French, Russian and German television channels dispatched their correspondents to ground zero.

In the beginning, the BJP government in Karnataka sought to play it down but as the footage began being telecast it was forced to round up seventeen leaders and members of the Sene by the evening of 26 January 2009.[6] Muthalik, who was in Maharashtra to attend a Brahmin Sammelan at the time, justified the incident by claiming that 'girls going to pubs is not acceptable' and that 'this small incident' was being highlighted to 'malign the BJP government in the state'. He was arrested the next day as he entered Karnataka. This was followed by a few more Sene men being arrested in Mangalore.

Within days, however, all the Sene men, including Muthalik and Attavar, were granted bail. The Sene chief described their release as their victory. 'This is a victory for all those who are fighting against pub culture in Mangalore,' he said, addressing the media outside the court. 'What we have done in Mangalore is a big success story in our fight against indecency. We are thankful to our Mangalore cadre for everything they have done.'[7] Nearly seven years later while talking to me at his Hubli hideout, Muthalik rates the pub attack as 'the single most important' factor responsible for the widespread expansion of the Sene. 'Till the pub attack we had units only in north and coastal Karnataka. After the incident, the Sri Ram Sene opened its units throughout the state as well as several places in Goa, Maharashtra, Kerala, Andhra Pradesh, Rajasthan and Delhi.'

In early 2009, before the noise generated by the pub attack could subside, the Sene declared that it would not let boys and girls celebrate Valentine's Day. On 13 February that year, pressure from all quarters forced the Karnataka police to take Sene leaders across the state into preventive custody, including Muthalik. The organization's outrageous acts and threats had inspired a group of women to launch an unusual campaign against Muthalik and the Sene. On 14 February, while the Sene chief and many of his lieutenants cooled their heels in various Karnataka jails, 'pink chaddi' consignments were dispatched to Muthalik at his Hubli headquarters. In all, the Sene chief received 1500 pink panties from around the country. The campaign irked Muthalik so much that after being released he organized a press conference on 22 February 2009 to call it a 'perverted act'. He also declared that he had formed a team of twenty-five advocates to file defamation cases against the senders of the 'panties parcel'.[8]

Meanwhile the Sene's activities continued unabated, primarily in the coastal region of the state. On 15 July 2009, for instance, some Sene members walked into a Hindu wedding celebration at Mangalore and assaulted a Muslim guest for attending the event. They regularly targeted Muslim boys for merely talking to Hindu girls and tried to whip up passion on the topic of 'Love Jihad' – the so-called conspiracy of young Muslim men marrying Hindu women to convert them to Islam – through vicious attacks and propaganda.

The Sri Ram Sene's mask of morality, however, disintegrated in May 2010 when a six-week undercover investigation published in *Tehelka* magazine exposed its murkiness.[9] The report said that the leaders and cadres of this Hindutva organization were not committed ideologues who spontaneously transformed into violent law-breakers for a 'cause'. They were unveiled as cynical thugs who could be bought for a price to riot on contract.

For the story, a *Tehelka* journalist posing as an artist met Muthalik and asked him if the Sri Ram Sene would orchestrate a premeditated attack on his exhibition of paintings so that the resulting furore could spark public interest and help his paintings sell in India and abroad. Not only did Muthalik agree to carry out the operation for a price, he also connected the undercover journalist to Sene members, including the Bengaluru president Vasant Kumar Bhavani and its heavyweight in Mangalore, Prasad Attavar. Muthalik did not hesitate to pocket the ₹10,000 that was offered by the journalist as a cash donation for the Hindutva cause.

A few days after this, the undercover journalist met Bhavani, a realtor by profession, and secretly recorded the entire cynical conversation. The talk revolved around the specifics of the planned attack in Bengaluru and how its impact could be maximized. The two also discussed the money the Sene leader would be paid in return.

Attavar, whom the *Tehelka* journalist met in Mangalore, was caught on camera saying he was evading arrest as a warrant had been issued against him for executing the orders of an underworld don, Ravi Pujari. Pujari had worked with the Mumbai gangster Chhota Rajan and later with underworld kingpin Dawood Ibrahim before establishing his own empire. As an associate of Pujari, Attavar had been accused of threatening businessmen and builders in Karnataka's coastal region as part of an extortion racket controlled from abroad. Attavar was arrested six days after the *Tehelka* journalist met him for the first time; he was sent to jail in Mangalore and then to the high-security prison in Bellary. But he maintained contact with the journalist, who even met him when he was behind bars in Mangalore and Bellary, where he agreed to carry out the attack on the exhibition.

V

The arrest of Attavar in May 2010 yielded two specific results. First, it drove almost all the important leaders of the Sri Ram Sene in coastal Karnataka underground and dampened its activities in places where it was most effective. And second, it left the field wide open for the Sangh Parivar, which had been blocked by an overactive Sene in Mangalore and nearby areas. While the Bajrang

Dal quickly stepped in to fill the gap, the RSS sprang a net to bring back into its fold those members of Muthalik's outfit who were ready to switch sides. Since many Sene leaders could not have returned to the Bajrang Dal, which they had left to form their separate outfit, the RSS revived another of its affiliates, the Hindu Jagaran Vedike, an organization that had been lying in oblivion until then.

The breakthrough for the Vedike came around the beginning of 2011 when a prominent Sene leader in Mangalore, Subhash Padil, joined it along with his trusted lieutenants – Suresh Padil and Sharath Padavinangady. Subhash belonged to the core group of Sene members who had left the Sangh Parivar in protest against its brahminical dominance and had met at Walke's residence in 2006 to form a new outfit. And he had not left the Sri Ram Sene along with Walke when Attavar had affected a coup of sorts in 2007.

In Mangalore, Subhash quickly built up an image as a ferocious street activist but within the Sene his relationship with Attavar was strained. According to a report published in the *Hindu* in 2008, when the Sene tried to enforce a shutdown in Mangalore over the Ram Setu controversy, Subhash almost attacked two journalists who caught him vandalizing shops where owners had defied the call. At that moment, Attavar had slapped Subhash and apologized to the journalists.[10] Despite his leading role in the Mangalore pub attack in January 2009, Subhash felt that he was overshadowed by Attavar,

Sri Ram Sene

who claimed to have planned the attack. In fact, it was the ferocity Subhash displayed during the pub attack – captured in the TV footage – that gave him both stature and position in the local Hindutva world. It didn't take much time for him to earn the reputation of a ruthless goon for hire, sought after by builders and land sharks.

When Attavar was arrested in May 2010 for running an extortion racket, Subhash and some of his associates went underground for a few months before joining the Hindu Jagaran Vedike in February 2011, possibly to get protection from the ruling BJP government in the state. After lying low for a while in the Vedike, he resumed his activities and almost revived the RSS outfit in 2012. On 25 May that year, an FIR was slapped on Subhash along with contractors and officials of the Mangalore Special Economic Zone for assaulting the family of a farmer who had opposed the land acquisition. The assault left four members of the family, including two children, injured.[11] On 26 July 2012, Subhash's Vedike followers kidnapped and assaulted a Muslim boy and a Hindu girl travelling in a bus from Mundipu to Mangalore. The couple was later handed over to the police but no action was taken against the assailants.[12]

Two days later, on 28 July 2012, the Vedike assumed the Sene's notoriety as Subhash and his associates stormed into Morning Mist Homestay at Padil village in Mangalore and assaulted girls and boys celebrating a birthday. The attack, which seemed a cruel imitation of the Sene's pub attack in 2009, once again made it to national and international publications. The Hindu Jagaran Vedike indirectly claimed responsibility but did not forget to distinguish itself from the Sri Ram Sene.[13]

In an interview on television channel TV-9 on 1 August 2012, Jagdish Karanth, the Karnataka head of the Hindu Jagaran Vedike, admitted that the attack was led by Vedike activist Subhash Padil but refused to call it the handiwork of his organization. 'It is true that the leadership was provided by Hindu Jagaran Vedike activist Subhash who is from Padil… In the attack, there was no banner of Hindu Jagaran Vedike, and Hindu Jagaran Vedike is not responsible. The ones who expressed their anger were local people.' The VHP and other outfits of the RSS, while supporting the objective of the attack, did not forget to add that 'The Sri Rama Sene is not accountable, but we are a responsible organization and function according to our role in the hierarchy.'[14]

VI

The arrest of Prasad Attavar and the large-scale exodus of its leaders and cadres signalled a complete meltdown of the Sri Ram Sene in coastal Karnataka, though it was active in other parts of the state. In 2013, Muthalik, operating from his headquarters at Hubli, set about reuniting the members who had deserted the Sri Ram Sene. As a part of his revival strategy, he also began to develop relations with the Sanatan Sanstha, a prominent Hindutva organization in western India which, like the Sene, is technically not part of the Sangh Parivar despite being ideologically on the same page. 'With spirituality as a tool to promote Hindutva, the Sanatan Sanstha has been growing quite fast. Every year since 2012, it has been organizing an all-India conference of Hindu organizations at Ponda in June. I attended two conferences in 2013 and 2014 but couldn't do that in June 2015 because the Goa government has declared me persona non grata,' said Muthalik. 'The relationship has benefited both the organizations. We call sadhaks of the Sanatan Sanstha regularly to address our cadres.'

In early 2014, with the Lok Sabha elections looming, the Sri Ram Sene experienced a renaissance. Many of its former members were rejoining the organization. 'Between 2013 and 2014, Muthalik came thrice to me and asked me to take charge of the organization once again in the coastal region,' says Walke, who had kept his group of loyalists close through the years even though they hadn't engaged in any Hindutva street politics. 'To facilitate our entry, he even expelled Prasad Attavar from the Sri Ram Sene. Initially we were not sure but around the beginning of 2014 all of us started working for the Sri Ram Sene once again.'

By March 2014, Muthalik's revival efforts had turned serious, making him attractive to the BJP, which was looking to pick up every bit of Hindutva muscle anywhere in the country in order to sail through the Lok Sabha elections. But the inner politics of the saffron party put an end to the reconciliation.

5
Hindu Aikya Vedi

1

Another sip of black tea. Another pause. Then another whispered explanation in Malayalam by one of the men flanking her. 'For much of the past centuries,' booms out the voice of K.P. Sasikala Teacher, the president of the Hindu Aikya Vedi (HAV), 'the Hindus of Kerala have suffered because there has been a planned effort to wipe them out. Earlier, Muslims and Christians used to do this with swords, now they are doing this with a smile on their face.' She then relapses into yet another pause, apparently waiting for applause. And there is always applause. The men almost seem to believe that she can make Kerala favourable for their politics through her teachings.[1]

Within the HAV, the RSS wing set up to prepare the ground for the BJP's Hindutva politics in Kerala, there is absolutely nobody who can match Sasikala's oratory skills. But when it comes to tackling tricky political questions, as in a formal interview, she needs constant support. The men who provide her this support – apart from regular doses of encouragement through applause – are trusted activists of the RSS. They stay close and whisper in her ear every time she looks around for an answer. The dais, however, changes her completely – it is there that she engages in the unrestrained pursuit of the Hindutva agenda, pushing it furiously and stubbornly.

Sasikala's rhetorical flourishes and overdramatic pauses – especially when delivered in the course of regular conversation – often give the sense of a performance which has been delivered many times before. This is appropriate because her public life since she joined the HAV in 2003 has been an act based on a script written for her by the RSS. The Hindutva outfit gave her the presidentship of the organization. It had great faith in her ability to pulverize Kerala society so that the BJP could sail through in a state hitherto known for its two-party politics: between the Communist Party of India – Marxist [CPI(M)]-led Left Democratic Front (LDF) and the Congress-led United Democratic Front.

As a result, she is the most sought after person for any meeting organized by Hindutva outfits in the state. However, as a native, she prefers to concentrate on the South Malabar region comprising the districts of Palakkad, Thrissur and Malappuram. In 1981 Sasikala became a primary school teacher at the Pattambi subdivision of Palakkad, and in 1993 she was promoted to a government high school where she taught social studies (history was her favourite subject). Sasikala joined the HAV as one of its vice presidents in 2003, when it had been relaunched and given an organizational structure by the RSS. In 2007, she was made its president – a post she continues to hold. As a leader of the HAV, she would like to be thought of not so much as a participant in politics but as a participant in 'public life', which she entered because of her 'Hindu feelings'.

Sasikala's speeches are clearly aimed at polarizing society on communal lines. She, however, insists that she uses her oratory for the 'awakening' of Hindus. Interestingly, she employs the Valluvanadan dialect to deliver her speeches; this is in vogue primarily among brahmins and other upper castes in the Valluvanadu region, which consists of parts of the Palakkad, Thrissur and Malappuram districts. Her critics feel that her speeches, both in content and form, represent an attempt of the upper castes, especially brahmins, to recapture the political supremacy they once wielded in the past.

Though almost every speech of Sasikala is pointedly divisive, some of them are shockingly brazen. Take, for instance, her speech attacking the then Kerala minister of cooperation and devaswom, G. Sudhakaran, who had made a request to the management of the famous Guruvayur Temple to consider allowing the entry of the renowned singer K.J. Yesudas, a Christian. 'Will he [Sudhakaran] write a similar letter to the authorities of Saudi Arabia urging them to allow Yesudas to visit Mecca? Will he dare to do that?' Sasikala asked in one of her most controversial speeches delivered soon after she became the HAV president.[2] Here's another example:

In 1921, when a group of Muslims [Moplah] went berserk in Malabar, Hindus ran away leaving behind everything – their houses, their wealth, their temples. It was a shameful chapter in the history of Kerala. Times have changed now. In Marad, when eight people died and fifteen others got seriously injured, the Hindus did not flee. They stood firm. That courage did not come automatically. It was the disciplined and concerted effort of the RSS which gave Hindus that courage. Similarly, in the 1950s, when Sabarimala temple was burnt to ashes by Christian fundamentalists, Hindus could do nothing except pray for Lord Ayyappa to chop off the hands of those who had done this. At that time they could just pray because the RSS had only begun its activities in Kerala. But in the 1980s, when a cross suddenly emerged in Sabarimala forests, Hindus did not shed tears in front of that cross. They prayed to Lord Ayyappa and organized themselves and plucked the cross and threw it away. Again this was not courage that Hindus had gained automatically over the years. This was the result of the organized work of the RSS to protect Hindu swabhiman.[3]

Despite being a teacher of history Sasikala simply does not bother about historical facts when she sets out to do her rabble-rousing. For instance, it was not a communal riot but a peasant uprising that took place in Malabar. Researchers have established convincingly that

Hindu Aikya Vedi

in 1921, the Muslim peasants of the region, known as the Moplahs, rose against their landlords: the Namboodiris and the Nairs. This resistance to extreme forms of exploitation by upper-caste landlords was suppressed and given a communal colour by the British. Why else would the very first batch of Moplah prisoners include a Namboodiri and four Nairs?[4]

Sasikala's speeches have earned her a lot of admirers who call her 'Jhansi ki Rani' after the valiant queen who fought the British. But the majority of Malayalis see her as a figure of ridicule, dubbing her 'Vishkala' because of the 'vish' or venom she spews in her speeches.

Away from podiums and audiences, she is not quite as articulate. She fumbles when asked if she would contest elections. 'No, no, no, I'm not fit for politics,' she says instantly and then pauses and looks around, realizing that there is something amiss in her reply. When she receives another whispered explanation from one of her RSS associates, she regains ground quickly. 'I am a disciplined worker of the Sangh. When the Sangh asked me to work for the Hindu Aikya Vedi, I did so without questioning it. If the Sangh asks me to contest [an] election, I will do that readily. After all, I did contest [the] election in 1996 from Pattambi as a BJP candidate. I was not a member of the BJP that time. I contested because the Sangh had asked me to do so. I was not in politics then, just as I am not in politics today.' She lost the Pattambi election so miserably that she had vowed not to ever contest again.

II

All Hindutva politics in Kerala – practised by the HAV or any other RSS outfit – emanates from the state's Sangh headquarters at Kochi. This is what Kummanam Rajashekharan, the general secretary of the HAV, tells me during a lengthy interview at the RSS office.[5] Rajashekharan, who has a soft face and an equally soft voice, has been the pivot of the organization that projects Sasikala as its mascot. The two HAV leaders have little in common but this hasn't come in the way of a cordial relationship. They certainly share similar prejudices against minorities as well as a commitment to the Sangh Parivar.

Rajashekharan cannot deliver galvanizing speeches but unlike Sasikala he is an astute politician adept at handling all kinds of questions. Perhaps that was the reason the RSS deployed him to set up and run an 'apolitical' organization with the objective of creating a political foothold for the BJP in Kerala. This was in 1992, in the aftermath of a communal riot in Poonthura near Thiruvananthapuram. A native of Kottayam district, Rajashekharan had started his career as a journalist. In 1976 he got a job in the Food Corporation of India, a public sector undertaking. 'In 1987 I left the job and became an RSS pracharak,' he says. 'Since then I have remained a pracharak.'

The Poonthura riots of July 1992 that claimed five lives was directly related to the Ramjanmabhoomi–Babri

Hindu Aikya Vedi

Masjid dispute. The Muslim fundamentalist organization Islamic Sevak Sangh (ISS) and the RSS reportedly played a central role in the conflict at Poonthura. The most important fallout of the resulting atmosphere of apprehension was the formation of the Muslim Aikya Vedi (Muslim Unity Forum) by the ISS and some other Muslim fundamentalist organizations, and the Hindu Aikya Vedi (Hindu Unity Forum) by the RSS. Neither of the two new bodies, however, received any popular support. While the Muslim Aikya Vedi faded into oblivion soon after its formation, the HAV survived – though mainly as a banner – with Rajashekharan as the key representative of the RSS in it.

'Soon after the Poonthura riots, the RSS organized a meeting of various Hindu religious bodies and sanyasis at Trivandrum, and a decision was made to set up the Hindu Aikya Vedi,' says Rajashekharan. Swamy Sathyananda Saraswati of Shri Rama Dasam Matham became the chairperson of the new body, while senior RSS pracharak Jai Sisupalan became its general convener and Kummanam Rajashekharan its joint convener. 'Throughout the 1990s and the early years of the twenty-first century, the main strategic value of the Hindu Aikya Vedi lay in coordination among various Hindu religious bodies and individuals,' says Rajashekharan. 'But the communal violence at Marad in the first week of May 2003 gave a new spin to our organization.'

Nine individuals were hacked to death in Marad, a

coastal village in Kozhikode district. According to the Justice Thomas P. Joseph Commission report, the riot that took place in May 2003 was primarily a consequence of the politically motivated killing of five people in the village in January 2002 and the Congress-led UDF government's 'unjustified delay' in the prosecution of those accused of the crime.[6] The report, which was submitted in 2006, maintained that of the 393 individuals against whom charge sheets were filed in 115 cases relating to the January 2002 incident, 213 were activists of the RSS/BJP while the rest belonged to the Muslim League, the CPI(M), the Indian National League and the National Democratic Front. It concluded that the delay in the prosecution of the accused was subsequently utilized by 'Muslim fundamentalists, terrorists and other forces' to capitalize on the grievance of relatives of Muslim victims and use it as a cause for vengeance against the Hindus of Marad.[7]

While Kerala was trying to come to terms with one of the worst communal incidents in its recent history, the HAV utilized the charged atmosphere to lay the foundations of its organizational structure in the state. 'After the Marad riots of 2003, the Hindu Aikya Vedi became a mass organization,' says Rajashekharan. 'We now formed district-level committees throughout the state. In course of time, we took our organization to grassroots level and formed committees in villages and talukas as well.'

For six long years there was no big emotive issue that

Hindu Aikya Vedi

could help the HAV turn its fortunes around. However, they persisted with localized agitations in several parts of the state. The dry spell ended in December 2009 when the National Religious and Linguistic Minorities Commission, with Justice Ranganath Misra as its chairman, submitted its report in Parliament. The commission recommended, among other things, the inclusion of converted dalit Christians and dalit Muslims in the list of Scheduled Castes. While the Left parties and the Congress welcomed the Mishra Commission report, the HAV, along with other outfits of the RSS, launched a nationwide campaign against it.

'This report became a turning point for us,' says M. Radhakrishnan, senior RSS pracharak, who served as the secretary (organization) of the HAV from 2002 to 2007.[8] 'We argued that if the government accepted the Mishra Commission recommendations, converted Christians and Muslims would become eligible to contest in seats reserved for Scheduled Castes. This would also allow the Scheduled Castes to share their reservations in educational institutions and government jobs with converted Christians and Muslims.'

The debate that had been stoked thus provided the HAV its first real opportunity to develop a rapport with many of the leaders of dalit and lower-caste organizations who were ostensibly concerned about their future after these recommendations were made public. 'That was a major breakthrough for us. Many lower-caste organizations started listening to the arguments of the Hindu Aikya Vedi,' says Radhakrishnan. 'Leaders of lower-caste organizations like the Kerala Pulayar Mahasabha, Sidhanar Service Society, Kerala Cheramar Hindu Mahasabha, Vishwakarma Sabha, etc. started coming to our programmes. We have tried to nurture the rapport with these caste groups ever since.'

Radhakrishnan admits that despite the HAV making substantial gains following the Ranganath Misra Commission report, the political results of its relationship with the lower-caste organizations will take time to manifest. Organizations – not just dalit outfits but even middle- and upper-caste ones – have played a significant role in the politics of Kerala. It remains to be seen whether they match the expectations of Radhakrishnan and the Sangh Parivar in recasting the state's politics along communal lines.

III

If there is a single issue that has kept the HAV engaged all these years, it is the demand of the RSS that Kerala's temples be 'liberated' from the control of the devaswom boards, the autonomous bodies that manage nearly 3000 temples in the state. There are, in total, four such boards – one for the Guruvayur Temple and one each for temples in the Travancore, Malabar and Kochi regions. While the Malabar Devaswom Board manages 1337 temples, the Travancore Devaswom Board is in charge of 1240 temples and the Cochin (Kochi) Devaswom Board has 403 temples under its management.[9] These boards are governed by specific legislations which took shape in the particular historical contexts of their respective regions. The recruitment of employees in these boards is also regulated by the statutes formulated and supervised by the Kerala state government.

The RSS and the HAV argue that just as Muslim and Christian places of worship are run by the respective communities, the management of temples should be left solely to Hindu devotees. They do not want the devaswom boards to play any role in their management. They also contend that the income from temples reaches the state treasury and is used for the welfare of minorities. The truth, however, is that instead of diverting the incomes of the devaswom boards, which are autonomous bodies, the state government is often required to pitch in and spend crores of rupees on the smooth functioning of the temples. That Kerala's temples, unlike churches or mosques, receive massive donations and that the management and proper utilization of this income require responsible mechanisms are not factors that HAV leaders would ever acknowledge. Instead, they point out that, firstly, the government 'controls' the management of temples through these devaswom boards, and secondly, this statutory mechanism has come in the way of Hindu devotees, the main donors, from getting their due share in temple affairs.

'At present, the nominees of the government are running devaswom boards,' says Rajashekharan. 'Donations from devotees account for the main source of the income of these boards. Yet devotees have no role in the management of temples. Such a situation exists only for Hindus. Worship centres of Christians and Muslims are not administered by the government. It has given complete freedom to the believers of these communities.'

The HAV has organized demonstrations and dharnas, and filed cases in various courts and campaigned among Hindus to put pressure on the government so that temples can be 'liberated' from the devaswom boards. 'Our demand is to abolish all devaswom boards and pass a Kerala Hindu Religious Institutions Act that would bring temples on equal footing with the places of worship of other communities,' says Rajashekharan. 'It is not democracy unless you implement it in temples, too.'

Perhaps nowhere in the country have temples been as intrinsic to the political strategy of the RSS as they are in Kerala. The temples are rich and have large numbers of people visiting them every day. They are therefore seen by the Sangh outfits as a convenient launching pad for their politics in the state. Since the beginning of its activities in Kerala in the 1940s, the RSS has been trying hard to infiltrate the management of temples. The devaswom boards have, however, remained generally out of its reach and actually been obstacles to its project. The RSS and its outfits have, therefore, formed parallel bodies in the guise of protection committees in a large number of temples in the state. Theoretically these committees – called kshetra samarakshan samitis (temple protection committees) – are bodies made up of regular devotees, but they are invariably dominated and controlled by activists of the RSS.

Interestingly, unlike North India, where the RSS holds its shakhas in parks and open fields, in Kerala drills are held mostly on temple premises. This has often led to controversy because these RSS activities are hardly ever sanctioned by the concerned devaswom board. They are held primarily because of the backing of the temple's kshetra samarakshan samiti. In June 2015, the Travancore Devaswom Board told the Kerala High Court that it had not granted the RSS permission to organize shakhas on temple premises and that it had taken steps to stop the conduct of such drills. The board's submission was in response to a complaint alleging that arms training had been given in a temple under its management in the southern district of Kollam.[10]

The HAV, in its effort to put forward its argument against the devaswom boards, has even questioned the accession of the Travancore and Cochin princely states to India after Independence. The modern state of Kerala was formed from areas which were under three distinct governments when the British ruled India. The northern part of modern Kerala was the British Indian district of Malabar, which was attached to the Madras

Presidency. South of Malabar existed the small princely state of Cochin and further south was the princely state of Travancore. 'At the time of accession to India, the right of the administration of the state was handed over to the democratic government,' asserts Rajashekharan. 'The administration of temples was a different thing and it should have remained with ordinary Hindus. That is why we are saying that the right to administer temples should be returned to Hindus.'

The argument is bizarre but the HAV has kept it alive all these years. Simultaneously, it has also tried hard to conceal its real motive for demanding the 'liberation' of temples. It has made it look like a benign campaign devoid of any politics.

IV

Many independent scholars believe that the HAV's 'baleful influence' – the extent of which is still being debated – has become possible because of the presence of Hindu caste associations. These came into existence before Independence and have been politically active all through but in an informal fashion. A study in 1964 notes that in Kerala 'the high correlation between ritual rank and economic position has given caste a solidarity and a significance in its political role, which is unparalleled in the rest of India'.[11] When the state enacted a series of economic and social reforms in the following years, the caste associations continued to exist but the politics of caste appears to have been subsumed by the politics of class.

The LDF enjoyed the support of the lower castes and dalits, while the Congress was backed by a section of the upper castes, and its allies the Kerala Congress and the Muslim League with their majority support of Christians and Muslims respectively. Breaking this arrangement between the two parties was the central motive of the HAV when it was formed in 1992. But the RSS outfit has not been able to alter the existing socio-political arrangement in Kerala in any significant way. Even the advantage it might have received vis-à-vis the Left and the Congress on the question of the Ranganath Misra Commission's recommendations could not provide the HAV any concrete political opening in the state. Nevertheless, it has kept working on its agenda to create a Hindu vote by coalescing caste groups in Kerala. Even critics of the HAV feel that in the last few years they have managed to gain some influence over sections of upper-caste Nairs, middle-ranking-caste Ezhavas and lower-caste Pulayas. While Nairs are miniscule in number and have traditionally been in favour of the Congress, the Ezhavas and Pulayas have a substantial presence and have stood throughout with the Left parties.

In this, the HAV seems to have benefited considerably from the changing ground reality in Kerala. Education and a high degree of political literacy together with stagnant economic conditions and growing unemployment have resulted in discontentment and restlessness, a situation similar to what existed before the land reforms. The RSS, which has never fought for land reforms anywhere in the country, is now presenting itself through the HAV as a champion of 'fresh land reforms' in Kerala. 'Kerala's land reforms had several problems. Landless dalits and tribals were generally left out,' says Rajashekharan. 'In 1967, each landless family was given ten cents of homestead land. But now these families have multiplied and the land given to them fifty years back cannot accommodate all of them. We are, therefore, demanding that a fresh land reform law be passed and every landless family given one or two acres of agricultural land.'

Land matters, and so do the votes of the landless. Time and again, it has been pointed out that the land reforms of the 1960s could not completely resolve the land question in Kerala, where the overwhelming majority of dalits and tribals continue to be entirely landless. The reforms, despite being most comprehensive in India, generally did not provide any agricultural land to agricultural workers, mostly dalits and tribals. It was primarily a tenancy reform with the transfer of land to intermediate and small tenants that left out the vast masses of landless workers.[12] It also excluded the plantation sector and thus put a vast geographical area out of the purview of the reforms apart from overlooking the question of the landlessness of plantation workers.[13]

Hindu Aikya Vedi

Since most of the plantations were owned by Christians, the HAV has even found a communal angle in the Left government's land reforms. 'We have presented a charter of demands to the government,' says Rajashekharan. 'There is the need for fresh land reforms in the state so that the question of landlessness is addressed properly.'

The CPI(M) finds the HAV's demands ridiculous. 'The same kind of people who opposed land reforms so fiercely that it led to the dismissal of the Communist Party government in 1959 have today aligned with the Hindu Aikya Vedi and started talking about fresh land reforms,' says Professor V. Karthikeyan Nair, faculty member of the CPI(M)'s EMS Academy in Thiruvananthapuram.[14] 'The Sangh Parivar's appeal is restricted to a section of the upper castes and the rich. It knows that that won't take them anywhere, and so it is trying to attract the lower castes by doing all kinds of drama.'

Ironically, as pointed out by Professor Karthikeyan, it was the organization of the Pulayas, the Sadhu Jana Padipalan Sangam, that first raised the demand of land reforms much before it was implemented by the Left government in Kerala. 'This was because all the other communities, including the Ezhavas, had got some land. The Pulayas, Parayas and Korwas were treated as untouchables and were thoroughly dispossessed. They were agricultural labourers who had even worked as slaves until slavery was abolished in 1855.'

V

On 18 December 2015 Kummanam Rajashekharan was shifted from the HAV and made the president of the BJP unit in Kerala. The timing of this move from the shadows to the forefront is striking. It happened just months before the crucial state assembly elections in May 2016 so the BJP could harvest the crop sown by the HAV. The HAV's pretence of being an apolitical body vanished the moment its most promising catch – the Sree Narayana Dharma Paripalana [SNDP] Yogam, the Ezhava caste organization – agreed to enter into an electoral alliance with the BJP. Over the past century, in working for the social and educational uplift of the Ezhava community, the SNDP Yogam has gained a significant voice in the politics of the state.

The SNDP Yogam general secretary Vellapally Natesan's move to align with the BJP met with resistance not only from a section of the SNDP Yogam but also from other organizations following the ideology of Sree Narayana Guru, the social reformer and founder of the SNDP Yogam. Natesan's rivals in the community became vocal and the Sivagiri Math, a spiritual centre of the Ezhavas, got divided over the Yogam's approach. Similarly, the Guru Dharma Prachar Sabha, which was set up to propagate the teachings of Sree Narayana Guru, openly criticized Natesan and warned him against using the name of the social organization for political gains.

Hindu Aikya Vedi

On his part, Natesan, having decided to join hands with the BJP, organized a 'Samarakshan Yatra' from the state's northern district of Kasargod on 23 November 2015. The two-week yatra ended in the southern district of Thiruvananthapuram on 5 December 2015, when, in a massive rally, the SNDP Yogam leader announced the formation of a new party, the Bharath Dharma Jana Sena.

The concept of a Hindu vote bank, with the SNDP Yogam leadership forming a relationship with the BJP, now began creating waves in Kerala. The Ezhavas account for over one-fourth of Kerala's population. As the main beneficiaries of land reforms, they have traditionally supported the LDF. Two important leaders of the CPI(M) in Kerala – V.S. Achuthanandan and Pinarayi Vijayan – belong to this caste. The CPI(M) decried Natesan's tie-up with the BJP as antithetical to Sree Narayana Guru's teachings. Its state secretary Kodiyari Balakrishnan warned the Ezhavas that the RSS would swallow the secular Sree Narayana Guru movement. He also exhorted the community to resist the SNDP Yogam leadership's move to use the name of their Guru for political gains.

The Nairs, on their part, formally stayed away from any alliance with the BJP. Their caste association, the Nair Service Society, is opposed to participation in politics. But the inclination of a section of the Nairs to the HAV and the BJP was hardly a secret.

Though the BJP won only one seat in the ensuing polls

– its first ever in the state – the alliance it led substantially increased its vote share from 6.3 per cent in 2011 to nearly 16 per cent in 2016. No less striking was the fact that the BJP, primarily due to the efforts of the HAV, had succeeded, to some extent at least, in creating a new space for interactions among some of the caste associations in Kerala. The coming together of a section of the Ezhavas and the Nairs under the HAV umbrella was at odds with the caste-based antagonism that had created the state's socio-political constellations in the first place.

The SNDP Yogam was formed in 1903. The Nairs perceived the efforts of the Ezhavas to uplift their people as a threat to their well-entrenched position in the region. In 1905 in central Travancore, the Nairs opposed the admission of the Ezhavas in government schools.[15] They also opposed dress reforms, that is, the covering of breasts among the lower castes.[16] The Ezhava caste, conscious of its numerical strength, began to exert its influence in the reservation of seats in government services, the legislature and in universities.[17] Also, in opposition to the Congress, which they saw as Nair dominated, the Ezhavas supported the British Raj in an effort to gain special considerations.[18]

According to Professor Karthikeyan Nair, the caste organizations, especially those of the lower castes, were generally progressive during the nineteenth and early twentieth centuries because they were fighting social ills. 'But caste-wise, they don't have any role in today's society…they have lost their traditional relevance. They sustain themselves now through disruptive tendencies which are against democracy.'

VI

Despite being at the forefront of the battle against the RSS, which has often degenerated into the politics of targeted killings, the CPI(M)'s ability to develop arguments potent enough to counter the rhetoric of Sasikala Teacher and the HAV seems constrained by its many past failures.

For one, it was the CPI(M) that inadvertently gave Natesan, the powerful general secretary of the SNDP Yogam, an opportunity to build a favourable case for aligning with the BJP. At the time of the Lok Sabha elections in 2009 the CPI(M) kicked up an unusual row when it entered into an indirect alliance with the Peoples Democratic Party (PDP) led by the controversial cleric Abdul Nasser Madani. Madani had spent nine years as an undertrial in the Coimbatore blast case and was seen by many, in so far as his fiery speeches were concerned, a mirror image of Sasikala Teacher of the HAV. Apart from causing troubles within the LDF, this alliance was also interpreted as the CPI(M) lowering the flag of secularism in order to attract the votes of a section of Muslims through communal campaigning. Pinarayi Vijayan, the CPI(M) state secretary, went to the extent of sharing the dais with Madani during the campaign events in Ponnani.

The CPI(M) might have aligned with the Muslim hardline party to ensure a split among Muslim voters, who had largely been loyal to the Muslim League. But it created an opportunity for Natesan to justify to the Ezhavas, largely voters of the Left, his decision to tie up with a Hindu hardline party.

In September 2015, CPI(M) leaders and cadres participated in processions held on the occasion of Sri Krishna Jayanti in Kannur, considered Kerala's Marxist capital.[19] The party leadership claimed that the processions were not meant to celebrate Janmashtami but to mark the conclusion of the Onam festival. But commentators interpreted this programme, held in the name of the party's feeder outfit Bala Sangam, as part of a desperate bid to check the massive drain of its sympathizers to the BJP. This took place in the backdrop of reports indicating that the CPI(M) had been steadily losing its Hindu support bases in its 'party villages' in the district.

The CPI(M) has tapped on Hindu religious sensibilities in the past too. In 1989, during the party's thirteenth congress, several posters and other publicity materials invoking Hindu religious symbols were seen in parts of Thiruvananthapuram. In one of those posters, E.M.S. Namboodiripad was shown as the god Krishna, steering a chariot with a copy of *Das Kapital* instead of the Pandava prince Arjuna.[20] The stage at the Shanghumukham beach where party leaders addressed a huge rally on the concluding day of the congress partly resembled a Hindu temple and partly the Kremlin.[21]

The CPI(M) could argue that these minor deviations yielded major benefits in the party's fight to restrict the RSS to the margins of Kerala politics. The mixed messages with regard to secularism might have helped the CPI(M) get short-term benefits but also contributed to the emergence of the concept of a Hindu vote in Kerala.

Even though the concept is still nebulous, its very existence even at the level of perception is a matter of concern for a state hitherto known for its secular and progressive politics. The popularity of Kummanam Rajashekharan's door-to-door campaign and Sasikala Teacher's speeches ahead of the 2016 assembly elections show that the RSS has gained the critical mass to openly pursue its Hindutva agenda – due to the activities of the HAV and the failures of its secular rivals.

Though the exploitation of religious sensibilities has fomented unrest in the state, there are deeper factors at play, such as the failure of successive state governments to complete the process of land reforms. The land reforms of the 1950s and 1960s had greatly improved the living standards of the state's disenfranchised lower strata. But the gains made in those decades have begun to vanish or become meaningless. If corrective steps to address the threat of impoverishment are not taken fast, people might start listening seriously to the tirades of Sasikala.

6

Abhinav Bharat

I

A small group of mourners stood silently as the priest chanted mantras around the body of Himani Savarkar, the niece of Nathuram Godse and the widow of V.D. Savarkar's nephew. Satyeki Savarkar, the son of the deceased, followed the priest closely. It was early on 12 October 2015 and the incessant rains of the previous night had given way to a bright morning sun. At the end of the rites, the body was gently laid inside the electric furnace while the chanting of mantras continued, the scent of camphor drifting in the air. The priest then pulled down the iron shutter of the furnace and led Satyeki outside the central chamber of Pune's Vaikunth Electric Crematorium.[1] Behind them were mostly members of the Abhinav Bharat, a close-knit Hindutva outfit facing a series of terror charges.

These mourners began to disperse in silence. The death of Himani had snapped the living link they had had with two historical figures, both of whom they claimed as a source of inspiration and a role model.

Himani was the daughter of Gopal Godse, the younger brother of Nathuram Godse – a Hindu fanatic who killed

Mahatma Gandhi on 30 January 1948 and was hanged along with his accomplice Narayan Apte on 15 November 1949. Gopal, one of the conspirators in the assassination, was imprisoned. Himani was less than a year old when her father was picked up from their residence in Pune and sentenced to eighteen years in prison. In 1964 Gopal was released but arrested again a month later under the Defence of India Act and kept in jail for one more year.

Himani could not have come to represent the joint legacy of Godse and Savarkar had she not married the son of Narayan Savarkar, the younger brother of V.D. Savarkar, the supreme leader of the Akhil Bharatiya Hindu Mahasabha and the fountainhead of Hindutva ideology. Along with the Godses, Savarkar had also been arrested and tried in the Gandhi murder case. The case against him was dropped on 10 February 1949 for lack of evidence to corroborate the testimony of the approver. Later, however, he was indicted by the Commission of Inquiry into Conspiracy to Murder Mahatma Gandhi set up in 1965 under Justice Jeevan Lal Kapur. 'All these facts taken together were destructive of any theory other than the conspiracy to murder [Mahatma] by Savarkar and his group,' said the Kapur Commission report.[2] It was this double legacy rather than any of her political work that brought Himani first to the Hindu Mahasabha and then to the Abhinav Bharat, an organization formed in 2006 by a small band of highly motivated Savarkarites of Maharashtra. She was a professional architect who joined active politics only in 2000 when she left her job and returned from Mumbai to Pune. 'I had my practice from 1974 to 2000,' she said in an interview four years after quitting her regular job and becoming the face of the Hindu Mahasabha. 'In 2000, I decided to stop the practice because I have the copyright on all Veer Savarkar literature. I am its inheritor. So it was my duty to take care of it.'[3]

The Hindu Mahasabha, however, did not seem to have much to offer Himani. She contested assembly elections from the Kasba Peth seat of Pune in 2004 and from the Kothrud segment of the district in 2009 – on both occasions the voters snubbed her. In 2004, she got a little over a thousand votes; in 2009 merely 684. By the time she joined politics, Pune had undergone a drastic transformation. Although it still remained a Hindutva hotbed, any influence that the Hindu Mahasabha had had almost completely vanished from the city. The RSS, with its dense network of shakhas and the solid backing of the Sindhis (Hindus who migrated from the province of Sindh in present-day Pakistan), was in total control of the region. The majority of the Maharashtrian brahmins, who once formed the support base of the Hindu Mahasabha, were now the backbone of the RSS in Pune.

Nevertheless, Himani was acutely aware of the significance that history had bestowed on her. In 2008 when she got an opportunity to head the Abhinav Bharat, she promptly snapped it up. In fact, she thrived in her role. When members of the Abhinav Bharat were found involved in the terror blast at Malegaon, Himani Savarkar publicly justified it: 'If we can have bullet for bullet, why not blast for blast?'[4]

II

The origins of the Abhinav Bharat are shrouded in mystery. It is named after, and said to be inspired by, the secret society of students that Savarkar started in 1905 while he was studying at Fergusson College in Pune. That society believed in revolutionary violence, in turn drawing its name and inspiration from the Young Italy movement of the Italian revolutionary Giuseppe Mazzini. But when Savarkar got a scholarship for higher education in England in early 1906, he left India.[5] The Abhinav Bharat remained inactive for decades and in 1952, five years after Independence, the Hindu Mahasabha leader disbanded it.

Who revived it and how are not quite clear. In an interview given to *Outlook* magazine in November 2008, Himani claimed that the Abhinav Bharat in its new form was started by Sameer Kulkarni, who was 'a part of the RSS'.[6] The Maharashtra ATS has named Kulkarni among those who provided logistical support for the Malegaon blast of 29 September 2008 that left six dead and scores injured. It is believed to be the handiwork of the Abhinav Bharat. (There had also been a blast in Malegaon in 2006

Abhinav Bharat

but the case involving the Abhinav Bharat relates to the blast of 2008.)

When she was interrogated in connection with the Malegaon case, Himani told the police that she was elected president of the Abhinav Bharat in April 2008 during a meeting in Bhopal.[7] She also said that Sameer Kulkarni was working on the organization's growth in Madhya Pradesh.[8]

Other testimonies as well as the FIR drafted by the then Maharashtra ATS chief Hemant Karkare suggest that Lt. Col. Shrikant Purohit – who allegedly played a key role in the 2008 Malegaon blast – was the real architect of the Abhinav Bharat. According to some of the interrogations led by the Maharashtra ATS, Purohit started the Abhinav Bharat in June 2006 when he led over a dozen people to the medieval Maratha king Shivaji's fort in Raigad. 'We took the blessings of Shivaji Maharaj's throne and decided to name the trust Abhinav Bharat and prayed for its success,' a participant in that trip told the police.[9] Later, in February 2007, the group decided to register the organization in the form of a trust, and the official address given for the purpose of registration was that of Ajay Rahirkar, a resident of Pune who became the treasurer of the new body. He too is one of the accused in the Malegaon blast case.

The uncertainty regarding the nature and origins of the Abhinav Bharat almost seems like an exercise in deliberation. Even Himani Savarkar, despite heading it for almost seven years, conspicuously remained unaware of many of its facets. It is also possible that she chose to speak out only to increase the confusion surrounding it.

According to Milind Joshirao, a close associate of Shrikant Purohit and the spokesperson of the Abhinav Bharat, 'To blame her for being unaware of many aspects of the Abhinav Bharat would be unfair. She joined the organization late, and so she might just not be knowing everything about its origins. Who knows what the truth is? In order to establish the truth, you have to produce evidence that stands up in a court. And so far nobody has done that.'[10]

Joshirao was detained for nearly two weeks after the Malegaon blast. 'It was during that period of confusion [caused by the arrests in the wake of the Malegaon blast] Himani Savarkar came forward to speak to the media on our behalf. There was no formal meeting to make her the president of the organization, and that is why you won't find anything to that effect in the papers of the Abhinav Bharat,' he said. 'She became [the president] because she claimed [to be the president], and we all respected her decision because she represented the great families of Savarkar and Godse.'

It wasn't simply respect that the members of the Abhinav Bharat felt; they also felt gratitude. 'After I was released from detention, I went to her place and thanked her for taking the leadership of the organization in her hands,' said Joshirao. 'I also requested her not to make blast-for-blast kind of statements. I told her that such statements might harm our interests as the matter was sub judice. She realized her mistake and never made such comments again.'

Indeed, there was visible restraint in Himani's remarks after this meeting. In January 2009, she denied giving a statement to the Maharashtra ATS that she was aware of the Malegaon conspiracy.[11] In February 2010, after media reports started to link the Abhinav Bharat with the German Bakery blast in Pune on 13 February that year, she announced: 'Abhinav Bharat is not a terrorist outfit. The Maharashtra ATS has not been able to prove its involvement even in the Malegaon blast. Linking the Abhinav Bharat with the Pune blast is highly irresponsible and objectionable.'[12] Though it has to be said that the Maharashtra ATS had never tried to connect the organization with the explosion in Pune.

Despite all the investigations, the Abhinav Bharat has remained a mysterious, inscrutable affair. It is hard to ascertain whether the founder or founders meant to keep its origins unclear or it just happened that way. What this demonstrates is that the confusion regarding its origin and structure has acted as its shield, affording the Abhinav Bharat a powerful legitimacy within the larger political class that remains committed to the idea of turning India into a Hindu Rashtra.

III

The Abhinav Bharat would have remained mired in obscurity had it not been for the bomb blast on 29 September 2008 in the Muslim-dominated powerloom town of Malegaon in Maharashtra. The probe into this incident dramatically changed the terror trail in India. It was led by Hemant Karkare, who was subsequently killed in the Mumbai terror attack on 26 November 2008. The investigation unravelled for the first time a conspiracy by right-wing Hindu groups – in particular, the Abhinav Bharat – to spread terror in the country.

Although the Abhinav Bharat was a small, Maharashtra-centric outfit, the blast it allegedly engineered was a truly pan-Indian operation. According to the findings of the Maharashtra ATS, the plot was supposedly drawn up and fine-tuned over five meetings, with Lieutenant Colonel Purohit playing a key role in hatching the entire conspiracy. The first meeting was held at Faridabad during 25–27 January 2008. Apart from Purohit, it was attended by a number of his accomplices, most of them members of the Abhinav Bharat. Some important individuals who were present and who were also named in the charge sheet along with Purohit include retired Major Ramesh Upadhyay, Sameer Kulkarni, Sudhakar Chaturvedi and Amritananda Dev Tirth (who is also known under the names of Sudhakar Dwivedi, Sudhakar Dhar and Dayanand Pandey).

These people met for a second time over 11–12 April 2008 at Bhopal. This time, as per the Maharashtra ATS, Sadhvi Pragya Singh Thakur, a former activist of the ABVP, was also in attendance. The participants 'conspired together to take revenge against Muslims in Malegaon by exploding a bomb [in a] thickly populated area. Accused [Shrikant] Purohit took the responsibility of providing explosives. Accused Pragya Singh Thakur took the responsibility of providing men for the explosion. In this meeting, all the participants agreed and consented to commit the explosion at Malegaon.'[13]

The third meeting was held in the Circuit House at Indore on 11 June 2008. According to the charge sheet filed by the Maharashtra ATS, it was at this time that Sadhvi Pragya Singh introduced Ramchandra Kalasangra and Sandip Dange to Amritananda Dev Tirth as two reliable individuals who would plant the bomb at Malegaon.[14] A fourth meeting was held in the first week of July 2008 in Pune, where the Sadhvi asked Amritananda Dev Tirith 'to direct' Purohit 'to give explosives' to Kalasangra and Dange.[15]

Finally, in the fifth meeting, held on 3 August 2008 at the Dharamshala of the Mahakaleshwar Temple in Ujjain, Purohit was 'given the responsibility to procure the RDX' for Kalasangra and Dange. He, in turn, authorized Rakesh Dhawade, 'a trained expert in committing explosions and assembling Improvised Explosive Devices', to provide explosives to the duo at Pune, where they met on 9–10 August.[16]

Along with establishing the role of the Abhinav Bharat in the Malegaon blast, the Maharashtra ATS began to uncover new evidence linking Hindu communalists with many previous bomb blasts that until then had been considered the handiwork of Islamist groups. The arrest of RSS pracharak Swami Aseemanand in December 2010 offered fresh insight into the activities of Hindutva proponents in terrorist attacks around the country. In a confession before a magistrate, Aseemanand said that the 2006 Malegaon blast was also the handiwork of radical Hindutva groups as 'a revenge against jihadi terrorism'.[17] He also stated that the group led by the Hindutva zealot and RSS pracharak Sunil Joshi was behind the 2007 blasts on the Samjhauta Express as well as those at Hyderabad's Mecca Masjid and the Ajmer Sharif dargah. Some members of the Abhinav Bharat also figured in the group. Although Aseemanand retracted his statement later, the confession helped investigative agencies greatly in unearthing the sinister Hindutva terror network.

In early 2011, the Malegaon blast case of 2008 along with other investigations into Hindutva terror activities were handed over to the National Investigation Agency (NIA). The NIA was held up for a few years by a series of petitions filed by the lawyers of the accused. Later, especially after the formation of the BJP-led government at the centre, the investigative agency faced allegations that it was not moving fast enough because of pressure from above.

In June 2015, Rohini Salian, the special public prosecutor working on the 2008 Malegaon blast case, stunned everyone with her accusation of the NIA – the agency had asked her to be lenient with the accused, most of whom were members of the Abhinav Bharat.[18] In a detailed interview given to the *Indian Express*, she said 'over the past one year', since 'the new government came to power', she had been under pressure from the NIA to go 'soft' in the case. She sounded extremely pessimistic about how she saw the case proceeding in the changed environment. 'Maybe they [the NIA and the government] want to loosen it [Malegaon 2008 blast case] and ultimately lose the case because they cannot withdraw it.'

Salian's revelation is significant not only because she has built a formidable reputation over three decades of legal practice, handling a number of cases as Maharashtra's chief public prosecutor, but also because she was among the few with whom ATS chief Hemant Karkare discussed his findings in detail.[19]

Whether the case against the Abhinav Bharat reaches a logical conclusion is significant for two reasons. First, the message that nobody is above the law would function as a deterrent, especially for Hindutva groups and individuals who appear emboldened after the formation of the BJP government in May 2014. Second, it would take the wind out of the Hindu majoritarians by putting a question mark on their favourite strategy of stigmatizing minorities, especially Muslims.

IV

Even though the outcome of the investigation hangs in the balance, its nature and scope were unprecedented. The transcript of the set of meetings held by the members of the Abhinav Bharat over 2007 and 2008 is explosive. The proceedings were recorded by one of the participants (Sudhakar Dwivedi alias Amritananda Dev Tirth) on his laptop, and they provide us a glimpse of the Hindu Rashtra that is the ultimate goal of the Abhinav Bharat. The conversations, which are part of the charge sheet of the 2008 Malegaon blast case, delve into various issues ranging from a new Constitution and a new flag for the proposed Hindu Rashtra, to the justification of bomb blasts and the Abhinav Bharat's cordial relations with the RSS and the BJP.

Here is an excerpt from one of them:

LIEUTENANT COLONEL PUROHIT: We will fight the Constitution, will fight the nation; this Constitution is not ours. […] The only way is to knock it down […]

SUDHAKAR DWIVEDI: On the first page of the

Constitution it is written that the People of India have adopted this Constitution. How did this happen? On what basis could people adopt the Constitution? Was there any referendum? No. Was there any debate on it? No. How could then it be passed? How was this written on behalf of the people and who wrote it? [...]

PUROHIT: Swami ji, if this is so then we have to fight the Constitution; we have to fight for our independence.

SUDHAKAR DWIVEDI: We have an ancient science of administration. Our Smritis are the Constitution of our society. At present there are as many as 14 Smritis in this country. Collect them together [...]

PUROHIT: In this country we want to have Hindu Dharma or Vedic Dharma based on the Principles of Vedas.

MAJ. (RETD.) RAMESH UPADHYAY: This Constitution is not applicable to us, will not be acceptable to us; another Constitution will come into place; then Hindu Rashtra is established.[20]

But a new Constitution based on the smritis was not considered sufficient for the new Hindu Rashtra. The key architect of the Abhinav Bharat also proposed a redesign of the tricolour: 'The flag shall be solo tamed saffron flag having a golden border and an ancient golden torch.

Length of the flag [shall] be twice its width [...] There will be four flames in four directions on that saffron flag representing [four] Vedas.'[21]

In order to establish the Abhinav Bharat as the conscience-keeper of the new nation, the transcript shows Purohit arguing that 'wherever Abhinav Bharat is started, there should be a temple, the temple of Bharat Mata [...] That would give sanctity to the idea of nationhood.'[22]

Such language reveals utter contempt for the institutions of the Indian state and the laws of the land. At one point, some of the participants in the conversation, including retired Major Ramesh Upadhyay and Lieutenant Colonel Purohit, own up to the responsibility of having carried out some of the earlier bomb blasts that had been seen as 'the handiwork of the ISI'. At another point, Purohit makes it clear that anybody who came in the way of the establishment of the Hindu Rashtra would not only be 'politically excommunicated' but he would be 'killed'.[23]

The transcript also shows that the Abhinav Bharat leaders considered the BJP and the RSS as friendly organizations, but that they could not expect much from them in the short term. They found the RSS lacking not in ideology or agenda, but in modus operandi and 'immediate action'.

The dialogue makes it seem like 'immediate action' is what spurred Purohit and the others. And for that, they required adequately motivated men as well as sufficient funds. The Maharashtra ATS prised the lid off the Abhinav Bharat's money trail.[24] According to the charge sheet, Rakesh Dhawade, who 'was present in the oath taking ceremony of members of Abhinav Bharat at Raigad [or Raigarh] fort' along with Purohit and Ajay Rahirkar in 2006, belonged to an organized crime syndicate. He had floated a body called the Institute of Research and Development in Oriental Studies – Arms and Armour (IRDOS). An amount of ₹2,25,000 was given to IRDOS by cheque from the Abhinav Bharat's account at the instance of Purohit for 'facilitating his [Dhawade's] services to commit' the blast. The charge sheet also revealed that the Abhinav Bharat treasurer Ajay Rahirkar 'paid ₹3,20,000 to Rakesh Dhawade for procuring weapons at the instance of' Purohit.

Clearly, establishing a Hindu Rashtra and taking revenge on Indian Muslims for 'past acts of terrorism' were not the only factors driving the Abhinav Bharat. Rakesh Dhawade, for instance, was doing all this for the sake of money. The charge sheet points out that many of the others were also working for pecuniary gains:

> This Organised Crime Syndicate of Rakesh Dhawade were committing bomb blast since year 2003. The present accused have joined the said Organised Crime Syndicate and have continued their unlawful activities for their advantage [...] They have created an impression that they are taking revenge of bomb blasts committed

by the alleged culprits belonging to Muslim community. The pecuniary gains of the members of this Organised Crime Syndicate are explained above by way of collection of funds and distribution of the same to the members of the organized crime syndicate for various purposes.[25]

Ahead of the 2008 Malegaon blast, money was moving in different directions with the Abhinav Bharat as one of the nodal points. One such trail recorded in the charge sheet is about the sale of a firearm by Purohit. 'Purohit had delivered one firearm to Alok of Bhopal as per the instruction of Sudhakar Dwivedi. The amount of ₹80,000 is found to be deposited in the bank account of Purohit as the cost of the weapon.'[26]

A day before Karkare was killed on 26 November 2008, the ATS revealed that it was investigating several Pune-based industrialists for donating funds to the Abhinav Bharat. According to a news report in the *Hindustan Times* on 25 November, the ATS believed that Pune-based Shyam Apte was the Abhinav Bharat contact person who approached industrialists for donations, which were diverted and used to train cadres for terror attacks. The ATS also believed that Purohit was in close contact with Apte for the Abhinav Bharat's fundraising initiatives.[27] According to the report, Apte had networked with businessmen and industrialists when he lived in the United States, where he was actively working with the

Abhinav Bharat

RSS and other Hindu organizations. Around the mid 1980s he returned to Pune and got involved with Purohit and the Abhinav Bharat.

There were also reports that Ajay Rahirkar, whom the ATS identified as the chief financial controller of the Abhinav Bharat, had received ₹10,00,000 from various hawala sources.[28] The charge sheet mentions that he paid ₹3,20,000 to Rakesh Dhawade. In addition, he paid ₹3,98,500 to another accused, Jagdish Mhatre; ₹1,95,000 to retired Major Ramesh Upadhyay and ₹95,000 to Sameer Kulkarni.

Not all the money raised on behalf of the Abhinav Bharat was used for the organization's activities. A part of it, as the ATS found out, was siphoned off for personal use. Praveen Mutalik, who worked as Purohit's personal secretary for three months before the blast and who evaded arrest for nearly two years, is said to have used Abhinav Bharat funds to set up his own business.[29] He had fetched more than three lakh rupees from Purohit and vanished with the money after the arrests began. Mutalik, who is charged to have helped the other accused in assembling bombs and their fuses, was arrested on 31 January 2011 outside his shop (selling mobile SIM cards) at Gokak in Belgaum district of Karnataka. Even Purohit could not resist temptation and used over four lakh rupees of Abhinav Bharat funds to purchase a flat in Nashik.[30]

V

The Abhinav Bharat's terror links appear to have left the RSS and the BJP bewildered as they attempt to understand the implications of its actions and their unintended consequences. The top echelons of both the RSS and the BJP have maintained that Purohit and his associates belonged to a 'fringe group' which had never enjoyed their patronage.[31] It is notable though that the then BJP president Rajnath Singh in a statement said that the police did not have sufficient evidence against Sadhvi Pragya Singh and the other accused in the Malegaon blast case.

Yet the Abhinav Bharat's RSS roots are clearly visible. Sameer Kulkarni, who had asked Himani Savarkar to head the outfit and who had founded the Madhya Pradesh branch of the organization, was an RSS pracharak. Himani told the police on 26 December 2008: 'I met Kulkarni some one and a half years ago when he was working as a full-time member of the RSS. Since my house is next to Savarkar's, he would come often and I came to know him very well. Then he told me he would be in Madhya Pradesh to work for the Abhinav Bharat.'[32]

Retired Major Ramesh Upadhyay was also a prominent Abhinav Bharat leader with strong Sangh Parivar connections. Before joining the outfit he was the president of the Mumbai unit of BJP's ex-servicemen cell. No less significant is the political track record of Sadhvi Pragya

Singh, the first to be arrested in the Malegaon blast case. She had been a leader of the ABVP, the student wing of the RSS, in Ujjain and Indore until 1997. Thereafter, she joined the national executive of the ABVP before taking up sanyas.

The most prominent former RSS worker to have joined the Abhinav Bharat is B.L. Sharma, who won the Lok Sabha elections in 1991 and 1996 from East Delhi on the BJP ticket. An RSS worker since 1940, Sharma had largely worked with the VHP and had actively participated in the Ram Janmabhoomi movement. When he became disillusioned with the Sangh Parivar's inability to achieve the objective of 'Akhand Bharat', he even wrote a letter to the BJP leader L.K. Advani. He read out this letter at one Abhinav Bharat meeting: 'Akhand Bharat was a lost phrase until Savarkar ji revived and propagated it. But the Sangh kept this idea limited to itself. Jan Sangh [the political party floated by the RSS before the existence of the BJP] adopted it, but with the formation of the BJP it was sidelined.'[33]

It was Purohit who played a key role in drawing disillusioned elements from the VHP and the RSS and building the cadre base for the Abhinav Bharat. An *Economic Times* report calls him 'an expert at liaisoning' and further says 'Purohit had a unique sixth sense in identifying radical members of right-wing outfits like the VHP and then motivating them to join the Abhinav Bharat... His ability to attract talent from the VHP aroused the interest of the VHP leadership, compelling Praveen Togadia [the VHP leader] to fix a meeting with him at a Mumbai hotel in August [2008]. Togadia is said to have cajoled Purohit to quit the Abhinav Bharat and work along with him in the VHP. But Purohit flatly refused.'[34]

Purohit, in fact, was in touch with Togadia for quite some time. He even suggested to the VHP leader that the Abhinav Bharat organize the bomb attack and the Sangh Parivar claim responsibility for it. He reported this conversation with Togadia in an Abhinav Bharat meeting: 'I asked Praveen bhai that I would make the action happen but will you come forward to claim it? Will BJP come forward? He told me clearly that neither would come forward.'[35]

Purohit had great expectations from the VHP. 'If and when [VHP leader Ashok] Singhal ji [is] removed from the VHP it [will] become a headless chicken. A body without a head will remain and this is what the BJP wants. This wing should become ours. Do not oppose me on this. This will be our main weapon.'[36]

The Abhinav Bharat's relationship with the Sangh Parivar is an odd mixture of resentment and expectation, love and hate. Akin to Nathuram Godse's relationship with the RSS – on the one hand he admired its organizational network and on the other he resented its inaction at the time of Partition.

Though the important organizations of the Sangh

Parivar maintained a cool distance from the Abhinav Bharat after the Malegaon blast case, the RSS affiliate Bajrang Dal came out in support of the accused. 'Policymakers should be worried if Hindus were taking to arms because of the government's skewed approach to the war on terror,' declared the Bajrang Dal chief Prakash Sharma. He also admitted that his outfit was running training camps 'to boost their [Dal members] morale. The country would not get its Abhinav Bindras if there were no armed training for the youth.'[37]

The similarities between the Bajrang Dal and the Abhinav Bharat are striking. The Bajrang Dal does the Sangh Parivar's dirty work and the latter extends a helping hand when the former faces a crisis. Rohini Salian's revelation in June 2015 about the pressure on the NIA in the Malegaon blast case points to this very quid pro quo.

The extent to which the Abhinav Bharat can provide future service to the Sangh Parivar depends largely on the outcome of the terror cases in the court. As of now most of their leaders are behind bars, though the formation of the BJP-led government at the centre as well as in the state of Maharashtra in 2014 is seen as a good sign. 'But the case may take its own time, and one cannot be sure about its outcome,' says Milind Joshirao, the Abhinav Bharat's Pune-based spokesperson. 'When our cadre base started falling after the arrest of most of our leaders, Himani Savarkar came to us as a ray of hope. As a representative of Savarkar and Godse, whom we regard as our heroes, her presence ensured that we won't have to start all over again from scratch. We managed to retain at least a part of our cadres. Her death even before the release of our leaders is a blow, a huge blow.'

7
Bhonsala Military School

I

The Bhonsala Military School appeared on the radar of the Maharashtra ATS not long after the Malegaon blast on 29 September 2008. While investigating the chain of events leading up to the incident, the ATS found that some of the key accused had been closely linked with the school and that the RSS-run institution had provided some kind of critical service to the Abhinav Bharat ahead of the blast. This was unprecedented in the school's seven-decade history. The Bhonsala Military School claimed to impart military training to its students, and said that its curriculum was designed to prepare them for various defence service examinations. Even though the school had previously been accused of instilling communal sentiments in students, the sensational findings of the Maharashtra ATS made for an unpleasant surprise. Clearly there was much more happening on the school premises than its management was ready to admit.

In a meeting in Faridabad over 25–27 January 2008 – one of many held to decide and fine-tune the terror plot (see previous chapter) – Lt. Col. Shrikant Purohit of the

Abhinav Bharat told his accomplices: 'Whatever I have said today is in fact taken care of by the officers sitting there. The entire school is in my hands.'[1] Purohit had been associated with the school for quite a long time. In his late teens, he attended a special coaching class there for short service commission officer aspirants that may have helped him secure a commission in the Indian army.[2] In 2005, when he was moved to Maharashtra and given the charge of an army liaison unit – a military intelligence cell responsible for developing and maintaining links between the army and local communities – his link with the school was revived. He is reported to have organized training camps and meetings on the campus which were attended by dozens of people. One of them was held on 16 September 2008, a fortnight before the Malegaon blast. Major Ramesh Upadhyay, a former defence services officer, admitted to the Maharashtra ATS that he had taken part in three meetings with Pragya Singh Thakur and her accomplices on the Bhonsala Military School premises in Nashik to plan the Malegaon blast.[3]

Once the investigation into the blast picked up momentum and new facts emerged about the school, the secretary of the governing council overseeing its overall functioning, D.K. Kulkarni, sought to put the blame on the then school commandant, retired Lt. Col. S.S. Raikar. 'Purohit had served with the new commandant of the school, Lt. Col. S.S. Raikar, and so requested him to let the Abhinav Bharat hold its meeting in the school,'

Bhonsala Military School

Kulkarni said, insisting that the school had no links to political groups.[4]

On his part, Raikar, who retired from the Indian army as the head of a military intelligence detachment in Manipur, denied any criminal wrongdoing. Soon after being interrogated by the Maharashtra ATS, he resigned from his post in the Bhonsala Military School without citing any reason.

In any case, Purohit found the school so 'useful' that in one of the tapes seized by the ATS he talked about starting a military school in every state – where recruits would be given rifle training during the summer and which could be used to hide people in case of 'any police action'.[5]

A number of army men seem to drift towards Hindutva organizations after retirement. Possibly because the communalism at such places is garbed as nationalism. The Bhonsala Military School, with its curious combination of Hindutva ideology and military training, seems equipped to capture the imagination of such army men whose sense of patriotism can easily get mixed up with Hindu communalism.

'The Nashik school and its branch at Nagpur have maintained a pivotal position in the activities of Hindutva in Maharashtra,' a senior official in the Maharashtra ATS tells me in Mumbai under the strictest condition of anonymity 'because it has all changed' after the BJP came to power in 2014. 'These schools have also been acting as Hindutva's window to [defence] services. Even in the calmest times, they are an irresistible magnet for army men.'

But more than that, the Bhonsala Military School appears to have become an important training ground for the foot soldiers of Hindutva. In fact, the Bajrang Dal organized training camps in its Nagpur branch as early as 2001.[6] This came to light during the Maharashtra ATS's investigation into the Nanded bomb blast of April 2006. This blast occurred at the residence of the RSS worker Laxman Rajkondwar, whose son Naresh died while making explosives along with local Bajrang Dal leader Himanshu Panse. Four others – Maruthi Keshav Wagh, Yogesh Vidulkar, Gururaj Jairam Tuptewar and Rahul Pande – were grievously injured.

The ATS found out that Panse had held a training camp at the Bhonsala Military School's Nagpur branch, which was established in June 1996, six decades after the main institute at Nashik came into existence. On 15 November 1999, the Nagpur school moved into its new campus, a part of which was used to organize the Bajrang Dal's training camp in 2001.

This was confirmed by S.R. Bhate, a retired naval officer from Pune who had been associated with the RSS since 1996. According to an article published by the *Hindu* on 3 November 2008, Bhate, one of the trainers at the camp, told the police that 'this was no ordinary camp. People were trained in short sticks, karate, obstacle course, and weapons. It had retired army and retired Intelligence Bureau men imparting firearms training.' Bhate also told the ATS that it was the RSS which provided the trainers in various disciplines for the camp.[7]

As the charge sheet for the Nanded blast started grabbing media headlines, the chairman of the Bhonsala Military School's Nagpur branch, Satish Salpekar, denied that the institute had any role in training the terror suspects even as he admitted that the school's administrators were from the saffron fold.[8] He also admitted that the administration had given the premises free of cost to the Bajrang Dal for 'a personality development camp' in 2001. According to him this camp was not monitored by the school authorities nor did they have the names of the participating activists. 'As per our records, around 100 to 115 Bajrang Dal activists from all over India participated in the ten- to fifteen-day camp. The training was provided by their own people and it was conducted in an open space adjacent to our school which was still under construction. I am sure that no firearms training was provided.'[9]

II

The Hindu communal politics that led to the founding of the Bhonsala Military School draws heavily from the fascist pedagogical practices that Dr B.S. Moonje, the founder, encountered on a visit to Europe in the early 1930s. A key Hindu leader of Maharashtra and the political guru of the RSS founder K.B. Hedgewar, Moonje was the president of the Akhil Bharatiya Hindu Mahasabha from 1927 to 1937. He believed that Hindus were living under two types of domination: 'the political domination of the British based on their strongest of Machine guns and the domination of Mahomedans based on their aggressive mentality'.[10] Instead of countering the British, he identified Muslims as the principal enemy of the Hindus.[11]

This view had a large number of takers in Maharashtra, particularly among the brahmins. As pointed out by Italian scholar Marzia Casolari, during the Second World War and in the years preceding it, militant Hindu organizations 'seemed to uneasily oscillate between a conciliatory attitude towards British and a sympathy for the dictators' and were 'preparing and arming themselves to fight the so-called internal enemies, rather than the British'.[12] The need to fight against 'internal enemies' seems to have encouraged Moonje to learn about fascist curriculums. He was selected as the representative of the Hindu Mahasabha to attend the Round Table Conference of 1931. This enabled him to undertake a tour of Europe, which included a long stopover in Italy. After the conference, he first visited France and Germany and then stayed in Rome for ten days from 15 March to 24 March.

In his diary, Moonje describes his trip to Rome in great detail, including his visits to the Military College,

Bhonsala Military School

the Central Military School of Physical Education, the Fascist Academy of Physical Education, and the Balilla and Avanguardisti organizations, substructures of the Italian fascist youth group Opera Nazionale Balilla. The Mahasabha leader was particularly impressed with these outfits, which were – as Casolari says – the 'keystone of the fascist system of indoctrination' of young boys and girls. According to Moonje:

> The Balilla institutions and the conception of the whole organization have appealed to me most, though there is still not discipline and organization of high order. The whole idea is conceived by Mussolini for the military regeneration of Italy. Italians, by nature, appear ease-loving and non-martial like Indians generally. They have cultivated, like Indians, the work of peace and neglected the cultivation of the art of war. Mussolini saw the essential weakness of his country and conceived the idea of Balilla organization. [...] Nothing better could have been conceived for the military organization of Italy. [...] India and particularly Hindu India need some such institution for the military regeneration of the Hindus: so that the artificial distinction so much emphasized by the British of martial and non-martial classes amongst the Hindus may disappear.[13]

On 18 March, Moonje received a letter from the Foreign Office of Rome saying that Mussolini would meet him at 6.30 p.m. on 19 March at Palazzo Venezia, the headquarters of the fascist government. Moonje's entry of 20 March says he reached the palace well in time.

> The palace is one of the old historic buildings and has big halls. I was soon called in. Signor Mussolini was sitting alone at his table at one of the corners of one of the big halls. As soon as I was announced at the door, he got up and walked up to receive me. I shook hands with him saying that I am Dr Moonje. He knew everything about me and appeared to be closely following the events of the Indian struggle for freedom. He seemed to have great respect for Gandhi. He sat down in front of me on another chair in front of his table and was conversing with me for quite half an hour. He asked me about Gandhi and his movement and pointedly asked me a question 'If the Round Table Conference will bring about peace between Indian and England'. I said that if the British would honestly desire to give us equal status with other dominions of the Empire, we shall have no objection to remain peacefully and loyally within the Empire; otherwise the struggle will be renewed and continued. Britain will gain and be able to maintain her premier position amongst the European Nation[s] if India is friendly and peaceful towards her and India cannot be so unless she is given Dominion Status on equal terms with other Dominions. Signor Mussolini appeared impressed by this remark of mine.

Bhonsala Military School

Then he asked me if I have visited the University. I said I am interested in the military training of boys and have been visiting the Military Schools of England, France and Germany. I have now come to Italy for the same purpose and I am very grateful to say that the Foreign Office and the War Office have made good arrangements for my visiting these schools. I just saw this morning and afternoon the Balilla and the Fascist Organizations and I was much impressed. Italy needs them for [its] development and prosperity. I do not see anything objectionable though I have been frequently reading in the newspapers not very friendly criticisms about them and about your Excellency also.

SIGNOR MUSSOLINI: What is your opinion about them?

DR MOONJE: Your Excellency, I am much impressed. Every aspiring and growing Nation needs such organizations. India needs them most for her military regeneration. During the British Domination of the last 150 years Indians have been waved away from the military profession but India now desires to prepare herself for undertaking the responsibility for her own defence and I am working for it. I have already started an organization of my own, conceived independently with similar objectives. I shall have no hesitation to raise my voice from the public platform both in India and England when occasion may arise in praise of your

Balilla and Fascist organizations. I wish them good luck and every success.

Signor Mussolini – who appeared very pleased – said – Thanks but yours is an uphill task. However, I wish you every success in return.

Saying this he got up and I also got up to take his leave. I brought forward my hand to wish him goodbye but he said – Not yet, I will see you off at the door. He walked up to the door and warmly shook hands with me wishing me good-bye and good luck.[14]

According to Casolari, there is no Italian report of the Moonje–Mussolini meeting. She has, however, been able to locate 'routine papers recording Moonje's request for an audience, dated March 16, 1931 and the response of the cabinet of the minister of the external affairs, dated March 18'.[15] That he received a response from the foreign office of Rome through 'a letter dated 18th' has also been mentioned by Moonje in his diary. According to Casolari it was the British authorities who 'managed Moonje's audience' with Mussolini.[16] As to why the British authorities did so remains a mystery.

III

Back in India, taking his cue from the fascist regime's Central Military School for Physical Education, Moonje

Bhonsala Military School

established the Central Hindu Military Education Society (CHMES) in 1934. Its objective was 'to bring about military regeneration of the Hindus and to fit Hindu youths for undertaking the entire responsibility for the defence of their motherland, to educate them in the "Sanatan Dharma" and to train them in the science and art of personal and national defence'.[17] It was under the aegis of this society that the Bhonsala Military School was eventually formed.

M.N. Ghatate, a Nagpur businessman and an RSS worker who was in London at the time of the Round Table Conference and who accompanied the Hindu Mahasabha leader to military schools in France and Germany and parted before Moonje set out for Italy, says in his tribute to the man:

> On return from the R.T.C. [Round Table Conference], Dr Moonje started taking quick steps in the direction of the establishment of the Bhosla Military School at Nashik... He moved round the clock to collect donations from various chiefs of the states, mill-owners and such others and piled up lakhs of Rupees (Maharaja of Gwalior and Pratap Seth of Amalner contributed one lakh each). But more important was the sympathetic attitude of the Commanders-in-Chief and Viceroys of India which he had won by dint of his honest and sincere contacts and his dynamic personality.[18]

It was, however, not just Moonje's 'dynamic personality' or 'his honest and sincere contacts' that enabled his pet project. Part of his success in obtaining support from both the British rulers and the native chieftains and businessmen for his school was because the Hindu Mahasabha leader promised them what they secretly desired. Moonje assured the British of loyal soldiers who would be dedicated to the Raj alone, and to communally minded chieftains and businessmen he made no secret of the fact that, once established, the school would facilitate the militarization of Hindus.

Proof of this lies in his conversations with some significant people of the time when he set out to obtain their support for the proposed school. Many of these were recorded in his diaries. On 1 February 1936, for instance, Moonje met Lord Brabourne, then the Governor of Bombay, to ask for land for his school. The governor clearly did not approve of the proposal in the beginning as he had apprehensions that the boys trained there might join revolutionary nationalist movements in the future. Moonje assured him that the students would be kept totally away from politics and that the institute would strictly act as a feeder school to the Indian Military Academy in Dehradun. Here is a part of this conversation:

> GOVERNOR: You have very clearly dealt with the question but does it really mean anything at all? No [smilingly], Doctor Moonje, you can't escape the

point that it is a communal institution. Besides, it is a military school. How can I, as the head of the government, associate with it? The commander-in-chief may do it if he likes but the government cannot. It is a central subject. The central government will have to be consulted.

I SAID: It is a kind of feeder school to the Indian Military Academy. Field Marshal Sir Philip Chetwode, with whom I have worked on the Indian Military College Committee, was worried as to how the Academy will prove a success if there be no feeder schools where preparatory elementary training could be given to boys before they appeared for competition for admission into the Academy... It is this deficiency which my school is designed to remove and the Commander-in-Chief was very pleased when he knew I was organizing such a feeder school.

GOVERNOR: That's quite alright. Personally my full sympathies are for you... I know the advantages but after everything is said, we can't forget that it is a military school. Who knows how the boys will behave?

I SAID: This point had already occurred to us and we have decided to keep the school absolutely free from politics. It will be purely an educational institution and there will be no politics of any kind whatsoever. That's why, Sir, I have asked the C-in-C [Commander-in-

Chief] to be so good as to arrange that high-grade British officers while travelling between Bombay and Delhi may inspect the school once or twice a year.

GOVERNOR: But what is there in such inspection? You and I may have the best of intentions but who knows, when both you and I are dead, how the boys trained in the school, when they become young men in life, will behave when the Congress may start another revolutionary movement against the government. You can quite imagine how the situation will grow serious and pregnant with menace to law and order, if say, ten thousand boys trained in your school in the military training, were to join the movement. Here lies the responsibility of the government. You can quite now appreciate my difficulty.[19]

Eventually Moonje, with his pro-government track record, seems to have successfully convinced the colonial regime that the school would only churn out youngsters who would be loyal to the British Raj. That alone, however, was not enough; he required a huge amount of money to establish the school. And he secured it by exploiting the latent communal feelings of Hindu leaders and businessmen. In one of the conversations, recorded in his diaries, Moonje explains to the Dewan of Dhar as to why the school would have only Hindu students.

Bhonsala Military School

DEWAN SAHIB: It is alright, so far as it goes… But you must be national. Why should you not take Moslem boys as well?

I SAID: We do not mind taking in Moslem boys if they would put up with the special discipline of the school but they won't come to this school and a few perhaps who may come will make themselves a nuisance as they generally do and then there will be a most undesirable controversy and the school will needlessly get a bad name. These Moslems have a knack of creating troubles and then with the help of the British Government begin to dominate and be troublesome.

DEWAN SAHIB: Yes, yes, you are absolutely right. They are needlessly creating a needless trouble here in Dhar also, where there was no such thing before. We were living as brothers so long but since the last six months or so some Moslems from Delhi came and instigated the trouble in connection with the Bhoja Shala, which, they say, is a Moslem mosque and not the Bhoja Shala…

I SAID: Thus you have your own experience of Moslem nuisance…I do not want to have any such trouble in my school which is quite a new enterprise.[20]

It was not just distrust that Moonje felt towards Muslims. He appears to have been obsessed with the myth of 'internal enemies'. H.K. Joshi (also known as Appaji), an RSS worker and a close aide of Moonje, had a terrifying experience of this obsession in 1928 when the two visited Delhi for a common project. 'I was staying in the Maharashtra Lodge…and Dr. Moonje was staying in Birla Bhavan,' writes Joshi:

> On the morning of November 1928, I reached Birla Bhavan at 7.30 a.m. by previous arrangement to be told by Baliram, Dr Moonje's servant, that his master was asleep. I told him that I was asked to be in at that hour and, therefore, he should wake him up. This he refused to do. Thereupon I pushed back the door of his bedroom and entered. To my bewilderment, the Doctor sprang up in his bed with a revolver pointed at me. I shouted out my identity upon which he cooled down instantly, saying, 'Well done, Appaji. Otherwise, it would have been bad enough.' He apologized to me squarely upon which I asked him why he was armed, and what shikar he had expected to make in sleep. Fully recovered, he laughed whole-heartedly and said: 'You must know this is Delhi and I must keep in readiness against those who regard me as their enemy. I mean the Muslims.'[21]

There is no evidence that Moonje ever faced any threat or attack from a Muslim. Yet the anti-Muslim sentiment he nurtured all his life reflected in everything he did, including the school he founded at Nashik.

IV

Under the aegis of the CHMES, the Bhonsala Military School was established in Nashik in 1937 though it was inaugurated formally only in 1938 after the shift to its new premises. Moonje's decision to name the school after the royal family of Nagpur arose from his loyalty to the Bhonsalas and his desire to return to the medieval glory of the Marathas. 'Our family has a tradition of loyal service to the Royal Bhonsala House of Nagpur, which we regard as our proud heritage,' he wrote in 1938 to Maharaja Alijah Bahadur Scindia of Gwalior. 'The Maratha States are heroic relics of the Maratha Empire of India, of not very long ago and as such it is our sacred duty to aspire for the return of those proud days of our grandfathers and work selflessly for the same.'[22]

Moonje, a brahmin, might well have felt grateful to the Bhonsalas of Nagpur because the latter ensured the dominance of brahmins by granting them land and appointing them in administrative services. When the British incorporated the Bhonsala kingdom the privileged position the brahmins had enjoyed thus far was put in jeopardy.[23] This might well have been the reason for a section of the Maratha brahmins fanatically aspiring to revive the good old days. Such was Moonje's devotion to the Bhonsala family that in early 1946 as the nation geared up for the Constituent Assembly election, Moonje wrote a letter to Sardar Vallabhbhai Patel saying,

'Raja Pratapsing Rao is a representative of the Bhonsala Royal Family of Nagpur and that the Hindu Mahasabha is not putting up any candidate against him out of our feelings of traditional loyalty to the Raj Family and that the Congress also should not set up a candidate against him.'[24]

The founder of the Bhonsala Military School considered it not just a centre for providing military training to young Hindu boys but also an establishment to preserve and promote Sanatan Dharma. He named the school grounds at Nashik 'Ramabhoomi' (the land of Rama) and its cadets 'Rama-dandee' (the bearer of the staff of Rama).

According to G.B. Subbarao, a close aide of Moonje, the founder named the school premises after a shloka in the Ramayana. He wrote in 1972:

> After the defeat of Vali in the Kishkindha Kanda, there is conversation between Vali and Ramachandra, wherein Vali charges Rama with a series of accusations, after answering which the latter tells Vali that 'This land Bharat is mine – it is Rama Bhumi. You have no place here. So you should quit.' It is this verse, Moonje told me, that inspired him to choose the name of 'Rama Bhoomi' for his school grounds. It is significant not only for the Rama Dandi trainees whose object in life must be to establish Rama Rajya here eventually, but also for all the aliens who are to quit from here, as the

Bhonsala Military School

Britishers had done in 1947.[25]

Neither Moonje nor Subbarao identify these 'aliens', much like the 'internal enemy' left unspecified by Hindu communalists. Moonje's school was, therefore, entirely devoted to Hindus and implicitly against non-Hindus.

The school thrived and in a short span of time it made a mark among Hindus, especially those belonging to the upper castes. Moonje started living inside the campus and got around – in the style of a kshatriya – on a horse. He was unflagging when it came to raising funds for it. On 30 August 1938, he wrote to Maharaja Alijah Bahadur Scindia of Gwalior:

> The Bhonsala Military School is expanding in its activities; so is also people's demand for accommodation in the School. We must meet these immediate and urgent needs; otherwise the school may suffer in the reputation that it has built up in such a short time, but it is all a question of money. The only source of obtaining money so far open to me is begging and I am doing it to the best of my ability and energy. But begging after all is a precarious source of income. I am, therefore, now seriously thinking of giving practical shape to my idea of starting a Lottery for the purpose. If it is properly and efficiently organized, it may be a source of income even to a lac of rupees annually. The object of the lottery will be to provide financial support to the Bhonsala Military

School in its expansion into a college first and then into an All India University of Military Training.[26]

The school ran smoothly for almost a decade. Given Moonje's devotion, there was no interruption in the flow of students or funds. But it almost ceased to exist after the assassination of Mahatma Gandhi by Nathuram Godse on 30 January 1948 resulted in an enormous wave of resentment against the Hindu Mahasabha. In Maharashtra and the Central Provinces, brutal attacks on prominent Mahasabha leaders by angry mobs became common. Brahmins in these states became the target of popular anger because of their over-representation in the Mahasabha and the RSS. Moonje couldn't do much to insulate his school. He couldn't even move out of the campus because of the demonstrations. In a mood of bitter disappointment he expired on 4 March 1948, merely weeks after the murder of Gandhi.

V

When Moonje died, the Bhonsala Military School began to sink. According to Ghatate, the Nagpur RSS man who had accompanied him on part of the European tour, 'The money stopped flowing in and so [did] the students as there was no person in the school's society who would put in efforts like those of the parent of the institute.' Though Ghatate was also part of the CHMES, the RSS had distanced itself from the Hindu Mahasabha, including Moonje's school, after M.S. Golwalkar took over the Sangh in 1940. The parting of ways between Moonje and the RSS became most obvious when Golwalkar – merely months after succeeding Hedgewar – refused the Mahasabha leader's invitation to the Sangh volunteers to attend guerrilla warfare classes at the Bhonsala Military School.[27]

For some time after Moonje's death, there was complete confusion. There was no one to look after the school. The RSS had been banned following Gandhi's assassination and the Hindu Mahasabha was crippled. But after the ban was lifted in 1949, the RSS started to look for ways to move forward. The Bhonsala Military School, though in deep financial crisis, was an extremely promising institution from the point of view of Hindu communalists. It was then that Golwalkar started taking an interest in it. Ghatate, who had by then become a close confidant of Golwalkar, proved instrumental in the RSS's takeover of Moonje's school.

According to Ghatate, by 1953 the strength of the students had come down to fifty and the media had begun to report that the school would be closed down for want of funds and enrolment. 'I stepped in at this stage,' he writes:

> I requested the managing body to give me two years' time for my trial before the school was finally closed and assets

were handed over to the government. The management agreed to this. I moved all around, especially in Bihar, Uttar Pradesh, Hyderabad and other places and admitted boys from there. Gradually the number on roll increased to 150 by 1955. Maintenance grant was sanctioned by the Education Department and the sapling so fondly planted by Dr Moonje gathered strength by this manuring and has developed into what it is today.[28]

The Bhonsala Military School was thus revived. But the revival came at a price. With Ghatate acting as Nagpur's key aide in the whole exercise, the management of Moonje's school was silently taken over by men belonging to the RSS. 'The shift took place during the period between 1953 and 1956,' says Major (Retd.) Prabhakar Balwant Kulkarni – who witnessed the shift and who had been attached to the school in different capacities from 1956 to 2003 – in a detailed interview that took place in Nashik.[29]

Kulkarni had been an active member of the RSS since the late 1930s. In 1961, he cleared the necessary tests to receive a letter of commission to the Territorial Army, a non-professional arm of the Indian army consisting of volunteers who receive periodic military training so that they can be mobilized for defence purposes in case of an emergency. 'The Territorial Army is the people's army. That's why I could join it and remained a member of the

Bhonsala Military School

Sangh,' says Kulkarni, who was mobilized twice – during the Indo–China war of 1962 and the Indo–Pak war of 1965 – and rose to the rank of major before his retirement. He was in the news after he was detained for interrogation by the Maharashtra ATS following the 2008 Malegaon blast. However, he was let off after the interrogation.

'The Central Hindu Military Education Society had life members who used to elect the governing body of the Bhonsala Military School. Along with the revival of the school, the composition of the Society's life members also started changing. The new members who joined now were all RSS men,' says Kulkarni, also a life member of the CHMES. In his eyes the transformation is justified because it was the RSS who had played a significant role in reviving the school. 'The revival would not have been possible had the Sangh activists in different parts of the country not sent their boys to the school,' he points out.

In fact, his association with the school seems to have been part of the RSS's larger takeover design. 'One day in early 1956, Guruji [Golwalkar was fondly called Guruji by RSS workers] and Babasaheb Ghatate called me for a meeting and asked me to join the Bhonsala Military School. I agreed and joined the school as an instructor on 12 June 1956. From 12 June 1956 to 31 May 1988, I worked for the school. During this period I held several posts – instructor, supervisor, principal and commandant.

For five years between 1998 and 2003, I worked as the secretary of the Central Hindu Military Education Society.'

Clearly, by the end of the 1950s, Golwalkar, who had never been on good terms with Moonje, had taken effective control over the latter's school. Ghatate, the man who facilitated this, also proved instrumental in its expansion. He played a key role in establishing a branch of the school at Nagpur in June 1996. Two regional committees were set up to run the Nashik and Nagpur branches – while the former is spread over 160 acres, the latter is on a campus of over 30 acres of lush green land.

An RSS member and one of the early recruits to the college, Dr Vivek Raje says, 'In 1985, Babasaheb Ghatate decided that the school should now expand into a college. The same year [the BJP leader] Rajmata Vijay Raje Scindia laid the foundation stone for the college, which was formally started in 1986. It, however, could not function for the initial two years because the University of Pune withheld affiliation as it had some reservations regarding the military education in the college. Finally, the college got the university's affiliation in 1988 and started functioning. I joined the college in 1989.'[30]

Despite its chequered growth, much of the ideology of the Bhonsala Military School has endured. It still remains, as it was at the time of its founding, primarily a school for Hindus. Its curriculum stresses, as it did in the past, on Hindu religious instruction meant to instil the virtues of Rama among its students. On paper, the school does not block the entry of Muslim students and teachers. But Raje says, 'There is no teacher belonging to Muslim community in the school. Among students, too, there is hardly anyone belonging to that community.'

8
Rashtriya Sikh Sangat

I

The New Grain Market in Patiala is a lively place during the day. There is incessant noise and movement – people shouting, autorickshaws and tempos honking, cars squealing to a stop, carts trundling in and out. But the area quietens down after sunset, especially in the months of July and August when there isn't much agricultural produce to sell or purchase.

On the warm and quiet night of 28 July 2009, two men emerged from a car and vanished into the darkness of the market. A little later, at ten o'clock, Rulda Singh, the state president of the Rashtriya Sikh Sangat, pulled up in his Mahindra Bolero in front of his house at the edge of the market. The moment he stepped out of his vehicle, the two men re-emerged from the darkness and with calm deliberation shot him several times. The assailants then ran to their car stationed a few metres away and drove off.[1]

Rulda Singh fell down but before losing consciousness he managed to shout for help. His family members and neighbours came out immediately and rushed him to Rajindra Hospital from where he was shifted to the Postgraduate Institute of Medical Education and Research. He died two weeks later.

The murder looked like a professional job, quick and neat. There was no doubt that it wasn't a regular crime. This was confirmed not long after the incident when the Babbar Khalsa International, one of the most dreaded Khalistani outfits, claimed the responsibility.[2]

Rulda Singh's murder left the Rashtriya Sikh Sangat's members extremely uneasy. And with good reason: since the early 2000s the organization had become circumspect about its activities in Punjab. They tried not to annoy the Akal Takht in the slightest. The chief centre of Sikh religious authority had perceived the Sangat's work as an attempt to dilute Sikh identity. Rulda Singh was one of the most prominent faces of the RSS in Punjab and the state president of its affiliate the Rashtriya Sikh Sangat. His work, as that of his organization, was seen by many as an effort to undermine Sikhism from within so that it could be brought into the Hindu fold. This would help achieve the ultimate goal of the RSS – a Hindu Rashtra.

Rulda Singh had an 'unparalleled reputation' in the Sangh community. He had managed to persuade several Sikh separatists to give up their pro-Khalistan stance and return to India. 'Rulda Singh was also the general secretary of the BJP's NRI Cell. In that capacity, he travelled extensively to the UK and many other countries in Europe and North America, meeting quite a lot of

Rashtriya Sikh Sangat

those who had been blacklisted by the government for their pro-Khalistan activities,' says Avinash Jaiswal, the Sangat's national general secretary.[3] 'In India, he campaigned relentlessly for the removal of the names of Sikhs who had taken a pro-Khalistani position but faced no serious charges from the government's blacklist so they could return to their homeland. Perhaps his activities threatened the politics of some of the Sikh hardliners and that became the reason for his death.'

Jaiswal's speculation echoed the views of Dr Avtar Singh Shastri, another national general secretary of the Sangat and a close friend of Rulda Singh.[4] 'Rulda Singh was making a significant contribution to integrate Sikhs with the national mainstream – indeed, it was his role in getting the names of twenty-two people removed from the blacklist at the time of the Vajpayee government that led to his murder.'

During the 1980s and the 1990s, in the thick of the pro-Khalistani movement, India had blacklisted hundreds of Sikhs living abroad who had staged demonstrations in front of Indian embassies, made speeches against India and provided shelter to Sikh terrorists as well as those who were declared proclaimed offenders by courts and those facing charges of murder and bombing. In August 2003, following the efforts of the Sangat, the government of the then Prime Minister Atal Bihari Vajpayee scrapped the names of twenty-two Sikhs living in Canada and the US from the blacklist. 'The aim is to give them another chance to join the mainstream,' Rulda Singh told the media in 2004.[5]

Rulda Singh's actions probably threatened to deplete the support base of Sikh hardliners by luring away those who believed in the idea of a separate Sikh nation. Equally provocative was the fact that he was the leader of an outfit that stoked the fires of communal discord between Sikhs and Hindus. The Sangat's position was that Sikhism did not constitute a separate religion and was merely the sword arm of Hinduism. Given the context, Rulda Singh's attempts to court Sikh hardliners might have appeared to be part of the larger RSS conspiracy to absorb the Sikh religious identity.

II

The chain of events leading up to Rulda Singh's murder in 2009 had begun over two decades earlier. It was rooted in the formation of the Rashtriya Sikh Sangat in 1986, in the wake of the anti-Sikh riots that shook the nation. The riots – essentially an attack on innocent Sikhs by Hindus – had followed the assassination of Prime Minister Indira Gandhi by two of her Sikh guards on 31 October 1984. A total of 2733 Sikhs were killed in the communal violence in Delhi, most of them between 1 November and 3 November 1984. Sikhs were also attacked in several other Indian cities, including Kanpur in Uttar Pradesh, Bokaro

Rashtriya Sikh Sangat

in Jharkhand (then part of Bihar), Jabalpur in Madhya Pradesh and Rourkela in Odisha.

'All of us in the RSS sat up as the anti-Sikh riots had created a division in our society and threatened the national unity,' says Avinash Jaiswal. A native of Abohar in Punjab, he has been an RSS pracharak since 1960. 'The concern was so widespread that soon the RSS men in different parts of the country started discussing the issue with [the RSS chief] Balasaheb Deoras. We could no longer wait for things to improve on their own. So the Rashtriya Sikh Sangat was formed on 24 November 1986 with the sole purpose of popularizing the teachings of the Guru Granth Sahib and re-emphasizing the commonality in our culture.'

But was that the real reason for the formation of the Sangat? Although Congress men were involved in the riots in large numbers, it was not as though RSS activists were seen protecting the victims. In fact there is evidence that men belonging to the RSS and the BJP did participate in anti-Sikh violence at several places. According to a news report in the *Hindustan Times* on 2 February 2002, forty-nine RSS and BJP workers were named in as many as fourteen FIRs in connection with the anti-Sikh riots in Delhi.[6] These cases – ranging from arson, rioting, attempt to murder and dacoity – were registered following the recommendations of the Jain–Aggarwal Committee which examined the affidavits filed by the 1984 riot victims.[7] The committee had, in total, recommended the registration of forty-eight cases, including those against Congress politicians H.K.L. Bhagat, Sajjan Kumar, Dharamdas Shastri and Jagdish Tytler.

Not all the RSS or BJP men named by the committee were ordinary workers. 'In fact, one of the accused, Ram Kumar Jain…was the election agent of Prime Minister Atal Bihari Vajpayee when he contested the Lok Sabha polls in 1980. A prominent BJP and RSS worker, Jain's residence, no. 87, Hari Nagar Ashram, also doubled up as an election office for the Vajpayee camp.'[8] No less striking is the fact that in the Lok Sabha elections that followed the anti-Sikh riots, the RSS workers overwhelmingly backed the Congress.

Clearly the real reason for setting up the Sangat lay elsewhere and was not as straightforward as its office-bearers would like you to believe. There is evidence to suggest that the RSS floated its Sikh wing to push forth its 'Sikhs are Hindus' line by playing on the fear factor and taking advantage of the Sikh community's sufferings in November 1984. Proof of this argument can be found in the monograph which provides the ideological raison d'être of the Rashtriya Sikh Sangat. Published in 1985, *Hindu–Sikh Relationship* reiterates the old RSS line that the Sikhs are not an independent religious community, that they are part of the larger community of Hindus and that it was the British who conspired to keep the

Rashtriya Sikh Sangat

Sikh identity separate. It woos Sikhs as 'members of Hindu society' and denounces them for thinking that 'they were different'. It also blames this line of thinking for the anti-Sikh riots – a bizarre way of justifying the communal attacks of 1984. The RSS-linked historian Ram Swarup is the author of the monograph, which has an introduction by Sita Ram Goel, another intellectual given to the cause of the Hindu Rashtra. According to Goel, Guru Nanak was merely representing 'the Hindu response to the Islamic onslaught' and was by no means propounding a new religion.

> The response was two-pronged. While Hindu warriors fought against Islamic invaders on many a battlefield all over the country, Hindu saints and sages created a country-wide spiritual upsurge which came to be known as the Bhakti Movement. The message of this Movement was the same everywhere, based as it was on the Vedas, the Itihas-Purana and the Dharma-Shastras.[9]

Guru Nanak, writes Goel, was one of the Bhakti Movement's many saints who established their own 'seats and centres' in different parts of the country for the dissemination of their message. 'Guru Nanak established one such seat in Punjab. Those who responded to his call became known as Sikhs.'[10] He points out that the Adi Granth is regarded by the Hindus in Punjab as 'the sixth Veda' in direct succession to 'the Rik, the Sama, the Yajus, the Atharva and the Mahabharat'.[11] Though Sikhism does not share all aspects of Hinduism, he writes:

> There is nothing in Sikhism – its diction, its imagery, its idiom, its cosmogony, its mythology, its stories of saints and sages and heroes, its metaphysics, its ethics, its methods of meditation, its rituals – which is not derived from the scriptures of Hindusm.[12]

Based on his 'analysis', Goel refused to give the Khalsa the status of a new religion. 'It was only a martial formation within the larger Sikh fraternity, as the Sikhs themselves were only a sect within the larger Hindu society.'[13]

Ram Swarup, on his part, deals primarily with the British conspiracy to separate the Sikh community from its parent Hindu society by converting it into a distinct religious minority like the Muslims and Christians. Although he claims that the conspiracy was hatched and executed jointly by British officials, scholars and missionaries, he especially blames British administrator and linguist Max Arthur Macauliffe.

> He told the Sikhs that Hinduism was like a 'boa constrictor of the Indian forests', which 'winds its opponent and finally causes it to disappear in its capacious interior'. The Sikhs 'may go that way', he warned.[14]

According to Swarup, the literature produced by 'Macauliffe and others' became 'thought-equipment' for Sikh intellectuals who carried forward the idea of a separate Sikh identity in subsequent years. In his monograph, he calls Kahn Singh Nabha, the much respected Sikh lexicographer who assisted Macauliffe, 'a pacca loyalist' of the British, for authoring the pamphlet *Hum Hindu Nahin* (We Are Not Hindus) in 1898.

Swarup regards the Khalistani movement as a culmination of the process initiated by Macauliffe and the British government. 'In the last few years, even the politics of murder was introduced,' he writes, adding, 'Camps came up in India as well as across the border, where young men were taught killing, sabotage and guerilla warfare. The temple at Amritsar became an arsenal, a fort, a sanctuary for criminals. This grave situation called for necessary action which caused some unavoidable damage to the building.'[15]

He even goes to the extent of blaming the Sikhs for the violence perpetrated on them in 1984:

> The whole thing created widespread resentment all over India which burst into a most unwholesome violence when Mrs Indira Gandhi was assassinated. The befoggers have again got busy and they explain the whole tragedy in terms of collusion between the politicians and the police. But this conspiracy theory cannot explain the range and the virulence of the

tragedy. A growing resentment at the arrogant Akali politics is the main cause of this fearful happening.[16]

It is not clear whether the publication of this monograph in the aftermath of the anti-Sikh riots was a matter of coincidence or if it was a deliberately designed message to the Sikhs – that they had been subject to violence because they followed 'British conspirators' like Macauliffe and worked against national unity by underlining their separate identity. 'We can grow great together; in separation, we can only hurt each other,' Swarup concludes, as if issuing a warning on behalf of the Hindus to the Sikhs.

III

Hindu majoritarianism taking on the right to lay down the principles of nationalism was precisely what Sardar Hukam Singh feared. A Sikh Congressman of distinction, he had cautioned against it in his address to the Constituent Assembly on 14 October 1949.

> Sir, I might be accused of communalism when I sound this discordant note. But I hold that this nationalism is an argument for vested interests. Even the aggressiveness of the majority would pass off as nationalism, while the helplessness of the minority might be dubbed as communalism. It is very easy for the majority to preach

nationalism to the minorities; but it is very difficult to act up to it.[17]

Not only does Ram Swarup's argument promote Hindu majoritarianism, it also presents a distorted version of the history of modern India. Macauliffe, a prolific scholar who translated Sikh scriptures and history into English, is known for his deep understanding of and sympathy for the people of Punjab and their religious traditions. The fact that the British government extended no patronage to Macauliffe for his extensive research and translations, which the latter had to accomplish with the support of the Sikh community, is proof enough that he was not party to any colonial conspiracy.

In fact, in his desperation to arrive at a conclusion that suits the politics of the RSS, Swarup denounces one of the critical means to understanding Sikh thought. The six precious volumes that Macauliffe produced are important not just to explore the Sikh faith and history through the medium of English language but also because they record the interpretation of the Guru Granth Sahib as orally communicated by the Gianis – those learned in the Sikh religion – from generation to generation.

It was this distorted history presented in the 1985 monograph that bolstered the formation of the Sangat in 1986. The insistence of the RSS that the Sikhs are nothing more than a Hindu sect – advocated by the Sangat openly during the late 1980s and most of the 1990s – formed the theoretical basis for the new organization. The Sangat's propaganda material in its initial years openly carried the arguments of Sita Ram Goel and Ram Swarup as they appear in the monograph.

Rashtriya Sikh Sangat: An Introduction, a booklet in Punjabi published by the Sangat's office in Ludhiana after the completion of its first decade, reproduces Swarup almost verbatim as it explains the 'conspiracy' of the British government and Macauliffe to 'artificially' create an independent identity for Sikhs: 'Macauliffe told the Sikhs that they are an independent religion but Hinduism is trying to gobble them up. Hinduism is like a boa constrictor of Indian forests which first winds [itself around] small animals and finally causes [them] to disappear in its capacious interior.'[18]

It further claims that during 'the Muslim period', before the British created the grounds for a separate identity, Sikhs 'considered themselves Hindus' and their Gurus never thought of forming a separate religion. 'Now it is our responsibility,' the booklet says, reiterating the central point of Ram Swarup's monograph, 'to understand the root cause of the problem and to make people aware of the truth.'

For about a decade after its inception, the Sangat maintained a low profile in Punjab, focusing instead on pockets of Sikh concentration in other states. Therefore during this period the Akal Takht remained largely oblivious to its real motive. To the members of the community living outside Punjab – those battered and traumatized by the riots of 1984 – the RSS outfit presented itself as the body working to re-establish harmony between the Sikhs and the Hindus.

The Sikh Sangat, however, sought to take full advantage of the political shift that occurred with the formation of the Akali Dal–BJP coalition government in Punjab in 1997 and the BJP-led National Democratic Alliance at the centre in 1998. First it stepped up its activities in Punjab, and then in 1999, fortified by the might of the friendly state and central governments, the RSS outfit organized a yatra of about three hundred sadhus, mostly Hindus, to Amritsar. It was ostensibly to mark the tercentenary of the creation of the Khalsa order by Guru Gobind Singh, the tenth Sikh Guru, but its actual aim was to send the message that Sikhism was part of Hinduism.

While the yatra was led by Haridwar-based Swami Permanand Giri, a Hindu sadhu belonging to the VHP, it was coordinated by the Rashtriya Sikh Sangat president Sardar Chiranjeev Singh. The yatra started from Patna Sahib, the birthplace of Guru Gobind Singh, and culminated at Amritsar where it was welcomed by Sikh Jathedars including the chief of the Akal Takht, Jathedar Giani Puran Singh, and the head of the Damdami Taksal, Baba Thakur Singh.

'That event gave us a feeling that the Rashtriya Sikh

Sangat had largely achieved its objective,' says Avinash Jaiswal. 'It was as if the Hindus and the Sikhs had smoothly merged and become one entity again. There was a debate now, inside the RSS, on whether to continue with this organization or not. One section felt that since the Rashtriya Sikh Sangat had achieved its objective it should be disbanded. But another section insisted on the need to continue with this organization because there was still a group that believed in a separate Sikh identity.'

The event triggered a debate among the Sikhs as well. Though no Sikh body had objected to the manner in which the Sangat celebrated the tercentenary of the Khalsa panth or the participation of important Jathedars, there was resentment within the community. This became even more intense when the Sangat's yatra was followed by the distribution of pamphlets and questionnaires in schools suggesting that Sikhs were part of the Hindu religion. One of the pamphlets distributed during the tercentenary function refers to Guru Gobind Singh's *Bichhitar Natak* where he says that all the ten Sikh gurus were the descendants of Rama. As per the pamphlet, 'The followers of Lord Rama, Krishna and Guru Sahiban are not different but they are part of one society and that is the Hindu society. The entire Sikh sect is an integral part of Hindu society... The RSS is working to fulfil the objectives in the philosophy of Nanak and Gobind.'[19]

The matter was further complicated when the RSS organized general knowledge tests in schools and framed

Rashtriya Sikh Sangat

the questions in such a way as to link the Sikh religion and its symbols with Hinduism. A few questions touched on the RSS and were interspersed with those on the Sikh Gurus. The tension reached boiling point in December 2000, when the Sangat decided to organize a recitation of the Guru Granth Sahib in the Punjab temples.

Reacting sharply to the Sangat's activities and programmes, the new Jathedar of the Akal Takht Joginder Singh Vedanti issued a stern warning: 'Once again we warn the RSS and its affiliates that they must desist from publishing and distributing literature in which the pious religion propounded by Guru Nanak has been distorted. They better not test the patience of the Sikhs. Otherwise the Shiromani Gurdwara Parbandhak Committee [SGPC], along with other Sikh groups, sants and Sikh intellectuals, will have to launch an agitation against such divisive activities.'[20]

As for the Sangat's decision to organize the recitation of the Guru Granth Sahib in the temples of Punjab, the SGPC advocate Jaswinder Singh declared: 'The Sikh rehat maryada strictly forbids the recitation of the Granth Sahib at a place where idols are placed. Placing a pitcher, ceremonial clarified-butter-fed lamp, coconut, etc., during the course of the reading of Guru Granth Sahib is contrary to gurmat [the Guru's way].'[21]

Sensing trouble, the Sangat retracted its plan. But the differences were out in the open. It was around this time that Vedanti dealt yet another blow to the RSS.

'In its outlook the RSS is like Aurangzeb,' he declared. 'The latter wanted to convert everyone to Islam, either by sword or otherwise. Similarly, the RSS also wants to convert everybody to Hinduism. Its ideology is dangerous not only for the Sikhs but for all other religions.'[22]

IV

The backlash forced the Rashtriya Sikh Sangat to back off for a while. According to Raghubir Singh, former general secretary of the Sangat in Punjab: 'Our activities in the state were held hostage to the fear that if we pushed too much, then we might end up with something a lot worse. But if, on the other hand, we did not do that, then our whole exercise would become meaningless.'[23]

Persuading a community to merge its religion with another one is a complicated business. It often cuts unpredictable paths, and the anger it generates remains unnoticed and has the tendency to explode unexpectedly. Perhaps the RSS thought it could succeed in its mission simply by inventing a consensus through some superficial activities. But the indignation that resulted from the RSS's first round of undertakings in Punjab was such that it took nearly two years to make up its mind about the next course of action in the state.

In 2003, sensing an apparent calm in Punjab, the RSS decided to make a fresh overture through its Sikh wing. In its all-India executive committee meeting that year, the

Rashtriya Sikh Sangat

RSS passed a resolution asking its cadres and supporters to participate in large numbers in the celebrations marking four hundred years of the completion of the manuscript of the Guru Granth Sahib and its installation at Harmandir Sahib.

Responding to the RSS, the Rashtriya Sikh Sangat prepared a detailed roadmap for a nationwide yatra called the Sarba Sanjhi Gurbani Yatra. Scheduled to begin on 1 August 2004, it was to pass through the birthplaces of various saints whose compositions figure in the Guru Granth Sahib. Apart from the Sikh Gurus, these include saints like Jayadev of West Bengal; Namdev, Trilochan and Parmanand of Maharashtra; Bhagat Sain of Madhya Pradesh; Pipa and Dhanna of Rajasthan; Kabir, Surdas, Ravidas and Ramanand of Uttar Pradesh; Bhagat Beni of Bihar; Shaikh Farid of Punjab; Bhagat Sadhana of Sind, and others. The month-long yatra was to culminate at Amritsar on 1 September 2004.

'In March, we submitted a detailed programme along with the route map for the proposed Sarba Sanjhi Gurbani Yatra to Akal Takht for its permission,' says Raghubir Singh. A week before it was to begin, on 23 July 2004, the Akal Takht issued a directive, naming the Rashtriya Sikh Sangat an 'anti-Panth' organization which was trying to 'mislead' Sikhs in order to obtain their support for its 'anti-Panthic activities'. The directive asked the community and its religious bodies not to extend any support to the Sikh wing of the RSS. It was signed by the Patna Sahib Jathedar Iqbal Singh, the Shri Keshkar Sahib Jathedar Tarlochan Singh, the Darbar Sahib Granthi Giani Gurbhajan Singh, the Akal Takht Jathedar Joginder Singh Vedanti and the Damdama Sahib Jathedar Balwant Singh.

The directive was so forceful that it compelled the Rashtriya Sikh Sangat not just to abandon the idea of the yatra but also to back off on the literature that had hurt Sikh sentiments. In a statement issued soon after the Akal Takht's directive, the Sikh wing of the RSS, apart from announcing the suspension of the yatra, also condemned the pamphlets and literature that 'appeared under the name of the Rashtriya Sikh Sangat' which hurt the sentiments of the Sikhs. The statement was signed by the Sangat's all-India president Gurbachan Singh Gill, its Punjab unit chief Rulda Singh and its general secretary in the state, Raghubir Singh.

Later, in November 2004, the Sangat held a meeting in Delhi to review its experience in Punjab and chalk out a blueprint for the future. 'Participants discussed with a heavy heart the Rashtriya Sikh Sangat's inability to bring out Sarba Sanjhi Gurbani Yatra despite having made unprecedented preparations for it.'[24] A total of thirty-one office-bearers from eighteen states attended this meeting in which the members were asked 'not to get disheartened' and organize programmes in areas outside Punjab, particularly in the birthplaces of the various contributors to the Guru Granth Sahib.

Rashtriya Sikh Sangat

For a short span the issue appeared settled, with the Sikh Sangat lying low in order to avoid any confrontation with the Akal Takht. It also suspended all its activities in Punjab, except for Rulda Singh's meetings with hardliners living abroad. That did not, however, mean that the Sangat had given up its work in Punjab. After staying away from any fresh controversies in Punjab for nearly two years, in 2006 the Sangat's national president Gurcharan Singh Gill raked up the yatra issue once again, alleging that his organization had planned the Sarba Sanjhi Gurbani Yatra only after getting a 'green signal' from the Akal Takht Jathedar Joginder Singh Vedanti and that the latter had executed a volte-face when he came back from his foreign tour.[25]

This was the first time the Sangat had explicitly levelled the allegation that the hardliners sitting in foreign countries were dictating many of the decisions of the Akal Takht Jathedar. This was also an indication that they were actually watching the activities of the Sangat keenly. All this further soured the relationship between the Sangat and the Akal Takht and Sikh hardliners.

The verbal skirmishes continued, and the Sangat suspended activities in Punjab, focusing instead on Rajasthan, Jammu and Kashmir, Haryana, Delhi, Uttarakhand, Uttar Pradesh, Chhattisgarh, Madhya Pradesh and other states which had a Sikh population.

Therefore, when Rulda Singh was shot dead in 2009, there appeared no reason to disbelieve that it was commissioned by someone opposed to the RSS threat to subsume Sikhism. Those who knew Rulda Singh and his activities seemed to have arrived at this conclusion even before the Babbar Khalsa International claimed the responsibility for the sensational murder.

He had been the only recognizable face of the Sangat in Punjab because his frequent visits to the UK and other foreign countries and his periodic meetings with Sikh hardliners were the only Sangat-related news that appeared in the state media. Rulda Singh was the intended victim that night, and the killing was meant to send a clear and unambiguous message to the RSS and its Sangat.

V

We don't know who ordered the killing of Rulda Singh or who executed it on the ground. There were a few arrests but most of the accused were let off in course of time. No one has been able to find out why he was killed. We can make some assumptions, and there is also the unverifiable claim by the Babbar Khalsa International. And yet the murder unnerved the Sangat and brought it to a grinding halt in Punjab. For some time at least, its members and office-bearers lived in fear of random acts of violence against them.

'We realized that in Punjab we could not move at all. One possible way out could have been to tell the people that we were not the same as the Rashtriya Swayamsevak Sangh. But that we could not do because we share the same acronym. Simply by hearing the term RSS, people used to get our background even without knowing about us… About two years after the death of Rulda Singh, a proposal to change the name of the organization to Shiromani Sikh Sangat from Rashtriya Sikh Sangat was discussed in a meeting of the office-bearers in Delhi. But there was no consensus on it, and the name remained unchanged,' recounts Raghubir Singh, who had attended the meeting as part of the Sangat's Punjab delegation.

The murder of Rulda Singh had a deep impact on the Sangat members. Their fear began to dissipate only after the formation of a BJP government at the centre in May 2014. The reactivation of the Sangat began with a series of visits by the RSS chief Mohan Bhagwat to Punjab where he held closed-door meetings with the chiefs of several deras (religious sub-sects), including the highly influential Radha Soami Dera at Beas.[26] There were also reports of RSS activists organizing marches in the state's Malwa region where they openly sported guns, pistols and other weapons.[27]

The Akal Takht responded quickly. On 18 November 2014, a meeting of Singh Sahibs (apex clerics) presided over by the Akal Takht Jathedar Giani Gurbachan Singh cautioned against the increased activities of the RSS in Punjab, especially in the rural areas.[28] The caution had come close on the heels of the Sikh religious organizations calling for a religious and social boycott of Patna Sahib Jathedar Giani Iqbal Singh for sharing a dais with Mohan Bhagwat at a Sangat programme in August 2014.

The confrontation this time has spilled out of the religious arena. As the ruling Shiromani Akali Dal, which controls the SGPC by proxy, is in alliance with the BJP, radical elements in the state accused the Shiromani Akali Dal and the Punjab Chief Minister Parkash Singh Badal of first allowing the RSS to spread its influence in Punjab and then using the Akal Takht to raise an alarm against the Sangh's activities. 'Who has brought the RSS in Punjab? It is Badal. Who controls Akal Takht? It is Badal. Who has ruined Punjab? It is Badal,' says Bhai Mokham Singh, the convener of the United Akali Dal, a newly formed political outfit of radical Sikh groups. 'Badal's mock fight against the RSS has no meaning. Both are harmful for Punjab and both will have to go.'[29]

As religion mixes with politics, the people of Punjab find themselves trapped between the Sikhs who stand firm for their independent religious identity and those who fall in line with the Sangat–RSS theory of Sikhism being part of Hinduism.

Notes

1. Sanatan Sanstha

1. Basant Bhatt, priest at the Ramnath Temple; interview done at Ramnathi village, Ponda, Goa, on 28 November 2015.
2. Sheker Naik, former sarpanch of Bandora Panchayat, Ponda, Goa; interview done on 29 February 2016.
3. *Indian Express*, 17 September 2015.
4. Saurabh Lotlikar, social activist; interview done at Ramnathi village, Ponda, Goa, on 28 November 2015.
5. http://www.ndtv.com/mumbai-news/thane-blasts-convicts-get-10-years-in-jail-466099
6. *Mumbai Mirror*, 27 September 2015.
7. Deed of the Trust of Sanatan Bharatiya Sanskruti Sanstha, registered under the Bombay Public Trust Act, 1950.
8. *Sanatan Prabhat*, 27 July 2007.
9. 'From the fringes to the forefront', *Hindustan Times*, 26 October 2015.
10. 'From golden hair to pink toilet brush, Sanstha lists chief's divine changes', *Indian Express*, 21 September 2015.

Notes

11. Ibid.
12. Ibid.
13. Rahul Thorat, managing editor of MANS newsletter *Andhashraddha Nirmoolan Vartapatra*; interview done at Sangli, Maharashtra, on 26 November 2015.
14. Govind Pansare, 'What should be the approach of revolutionaries to religion' (English translation from Marathi by Dr Uday Narkar), in *The Republic of Reason: Words They Could Not Kill*, Sahmat, New Delhi, 2015.
15. Megha Pansare, 'Tribute', in *The Republic of Reason: Words They Could Not Kill*, Sahmat, New Delhi, 2015.
16. 'MM Kalburgi killing: The silencing of the reason?', *Indian Express*, 31 August 2015.
17. *Daily News & Analysis*, 29 February 2016.
18. 'Sanatan Sanstha Top Boss, His No 2 Questioned by CBI', *Mumbai Mirror*, 25 February 2016.
19. *Hindustan Times*, New Delhi, 26 October 2015, p.13.
20. 'For Sanatan Sanstha, defamation is a tool to weigh down opponents', *Hindu*, 27 September 2015.
21. Ibid.
22. 'Local outfit wants Sanatan Sanstha thrown out of the village', *Daily News & Analysis*, 1 October 2015.
23. Ibid.

2. Hindu Yuva Vahini

1. The FIR was filed at 5.25 p.m. on 10 February 1999 by Station House Officer B.K. Shrivastava, Kotwali Police Station, Maharajganj.
2. Dhirendra K. Jha, *Ayodhya: The Dark Night*, HarperCollins Publishers India, New Delhi, 2012, p. 31.

Notes

3. Justice Jeevan Lal Kapur, *Report of the Commission of Inquiry into Conspiracy to Murder Mahatma Gandhi*, Part I, p. 155, para 12B.10.
4. For details see Dhirendra K. Jha, *Ayodhya: The Dark Night*, HarperCollins Publishers India, New Delhi, 2012.
5. *The Statesman*, 13 June 1950.
6. Christophe Jaffrelot, 'The other saffron', *The Indian Express*, 6 October 2014.
7. Tanika Sarkar, 'Educating the children of the Hindu Rashtra', in Christophe Jaffrelot (ed.), *The Sangh Parivar: A Reader*, Oxford University Press, New Delhi, 2005, p. 197.
8. Christophe Jaffrelot, 'The Other Saffron', *The Indian Express*, 6 October 2014.
9. *The Statesman*, 1 February 1989.
10. Atul Chaurasia, 'The Yogi and His Tricks', *Tehelka*, 30 September 2014.
11. Sunil Singh, Uttar Pradesh HYV president, interview done at Gorakhpur on 26 January 2016.
12. Ibid.
13. Manoj Kumar, senior journalist; interview done at Gorakhpur on 26 January 2016.
14. Atul Chaurasia, 'The Yogi and His Tricks', *Tehelka*, 30 September 2014.
15. *Press Trust of India*, 7 February 2007.
16. *Hindu*, 13 March 2007.
17. *Indian Express*, 9 February 2014.
18. Dhirendra K. Jha, 'Ayodhya Shining', *Open*, 20 January 2014.
19. Ibid.
20. Talat Aziz, Congress party leader; interview done at Gorakhpur on 25 January 2016.

21. Parvez Parwaz; interview done at Gorakhpur on 25 January 2016.
22. The FIR was filed on 2 November 2008 at Cantt Police Station, Gorakhpur.
23. Maulshree Seth, 'On Yogi govt table, file on Yogi hate speech', *Indian Express*, 23 March 2017.

3. Bajrang Dal

1. Sharan Pampwell, state convener of the Bajrang Dal in Karnataka; interview done at Mangalore on 30 November 2015.
2. The name of the businessman who owns a shop in the City Centre mall (Mangalore) is not being cited because he preferred to remain anonymous while being interviewed on 1 December 2015.
3. Yugal Kishore Sharan Shastri, former convener of the VHP's Faizabad unit; interview done at Ayodhya, Faizabad, on 24 January 2016.
4. Peter van der Veer, *God Must be Liberated!*, *Modern Asian Studies*, 21, 2 (1987), p. 291.
5. Ibid. p. 298.
6. A.G. Noorani, *The RSS and the BJP: A Division of Labour*, LeftWord Books, New Delhi, 2000, p. 71.
7. Ibid. p. 71.
8. Thomas Blom Hansen, *The Saffron Wave*, Oxford University Press, New Delhi, 1999, p. 165.
9. Neeladri Bhattacharya (ed.), *Khaki Shorts and Saffron Flags*, Orient Longman Ltd, Hyderabad, 1993, p. 68.
10. Noorani, p. 77.

Notes

11. Pralay Kanungo, *RSS's Tryst with Politics*, Manohar, Delhi, 2002, p. 212.
12. Christophe Jaffrelot, 'Dal vs State', *Indian Express*, 3 September 2015.
13. Ibid.
14. Paul R. Brass, *Theft of an Idol*, Princeton University Press, 1997, p. 17.
15. Christophe Jaffrelot, *The Hindu Nationalist Movement and Indian Politics*, C. Hurst & Company, London, 1996, pp. 430-31.
16. Ibid.
17. Ibid.
18. http://vhp.org/vhp-glance/youth/dim1-bajrang-dal/
19. 'Loonies at Large', *India Today*, 8 February 1999.
20. See, for instance, 'Genocide in the land of Gandhi', *Hindu*, 10 March 2002; 'Godhra Victims, VHP Angry with Narendra Modi, *Hindustan Times*, 21 February 2011; 'Violence in Vadodara: A report', International Initiative for Justice, 26 June 2002, p. 10; Kavita Panjabi, Krishna Bandopadhyay & Bolan Gangopadhyay, 'The next generation: In the wake of the genocide (A report on the impact of the Gujarat pogrom on children and the young), Human Rights Watch, July 2002, p. 44.
21. After killing them, I felt like Maharana Pratap', *Tehelka*, 3 November 2007.
22. Ibid.
23. Ibid.
24. Christophe Jaffrelot, 'Dal vs State', *Indian Express*, 3 September 2015.

25. Dionne Bunsha, 'Organised Intolerance', *Frontline*, 13–26 March 2004.
26. Ibid.
27. 'A Call to Arms', *Outlook*, 15 September 2008.
28. Ibid.
29. *Indian Express*, Lucknow, 28 August 2008.
30. Ibid.
31. 'Ban against Bajrang Dal can't be sustained: NSA', *Press Trust of India*, 12 October 2008.
32. Ibid.
33. Christophe Jaffrelot, 'Dal vs State', *Indian Express*, 3 September 2015.
34. See, for instance, 'Muslims who converted will get ration cards, says Bajrang Dal', IndiaToday.in, 9 December 2014; 'We were misled into conversion in a Bajrang Dal exercise: Muslim families', *Indian Express*, 10 December 2014.
35. 'Bajrang Dal activists tonsure, parade man for conversion bid', *Indian Express*, 31 January 2016.
36. 'Bajrang Dal seeks complete beef ban, death penalty for defying', *Business Standard*, 21 September 2015.
37. 'VHP, Bajrang Dal offer to arrange lawyer for Dadri lynching accused', *Times of India*, 12 October 2015.
38. 'Beef row: Held Kashmiri students to save them from Bajrang Dal, says police', *Indian Express*, 18 March 2016

4. Sri Ram Sene

1. Pramod Muthalik, president of Sri Ram Sene; interview done at Hubli, Karnataka, on 29 November 2015.
2. *Indian Express*, 24 March 2014.

3. *Indian Express*, 25 March 2014.
4. Praveen Walke, state general secretary of Sri Ram Sene; interview done at Mangalore, Karnataka, on 30 November 2015.
5. *Deccan Herald*, 15 September 2008.
6. *Times of India*, 27 January 2009.
7. 'Mangalore pub row: Sri Ram Sene men get bail', IBNLive.com, 31 January 2009.
8. 'Pink chaddi campaign a perverted act: Muthalik', Rediff.com, 22 February 2009.
9. *Tehelka*, 22 May 2010.
10. Sudipto Mondal, 'The rise and rise of a Hindutva hitman', *Hindu*, 31 July 2012.
11. Ibid.
12. Ibid.
13. 'Communal policing by Hindutva outfits', People's Union for Civil Liberties and Forum against Atrocities on Women, Mangalore, September 2012.
14. Ibid.

5. Hindu Aikya Vedi

1. Sasikala Teacher, president of Hindu Aikya Vedi; interview done at Kaledi near Kochi on 4 December 2015.
2. https://youtu.be/E2wILWpuHeM
3. https://youtu.be/wk1bO3gM_bs
4. Sumit Sarkar, *Modern India: 1885–1947*, Macmillan India Ltd., Madras–Bombay–Delhi–Patna, 1983, p. 217.
5. Kummanam Rajashekharan, general secretary of the HAV; interview done at Kochi on 4 December 2015.

6. 'Marad Shocks', *Frontline*, 7–20 October 2006.
7. Ibid.
8. M. Radhakrishnan, former secretary (organization) of the HAV; interview done at Kochi on 4 December 2015.
9. 'They manage the wealth of the gods', *Times of India,* Calicut, 4 September 2012.
10. *Times of India*, 5 June 2015, Kochi edition. http://timesofindia.indiatimes.com/city/kochi/No-permission-for-RSS-to-conduct-shakha-in-temple-Kerala-HC-told/articleshow/47558696.cms
11. Robert L. Hardgrave, Jr., 'Caste, class and politics in Kerala,' *Political Science Review* (University of Rajasthan), Vol. 3, No. 1, pp. 120-6.
12. Dr K.T. Rammohan, 'Caste and landlessness in Kerala: Signals from Chingara', *Economic and Political Weekly*, 13 September 2008, pp. 14-16.
13. Ibid.
14. Professor V. Karthikeyan Nair, faculty member of the CPI(M)'s EMS Academy; interview done at Thiruvananthapuram on 6 December 2015.
15. Robert L. Hardgrave, Jr., 'Caste in Kerala: A preface to the elections,' *Economic and Political Weekly*, 21 November 1964, pp. 1841–1847.
16. Ibid.
17. Ibid.
18. Ibid.
19. 'Krishna, Krishna! Hurry, Hurry! Chant Marxists', *Pioneer*, 6 September 2015.
20. T.G. Jacob, 'Marxist Party and Communalism' (translated

from Malayalam), *Jayakeralam*, January–March 1989, pp. 41–2.
21. Ibid.

6. Abhinav Bharat

1. Satyeki Savarkar, son of Himani Savarkar; interview done at Pune on 24 November 2015.
2. Justice Jeevan Lal Kapur, 'Report of the Commission of Inquiry into Conspiracy to Murder Mahatma Gandhi', Part 1, New Delhi, 1970, p. 303, para 25.106.
3. http://www.rediff.com/election/2004/oct/06inter.htm
4. 'If we can have bullet for bullet, why not blast for blast?', *Outlook*, 17 November 2008.
5. Verinder Grover (ed.), *V.D. Savarkar*, Deep & Deep Publications, New Delhi, 1993, p. 428.
6. 'If we can have bullet for bullet, why not blast for blast?', *Outlook*, 17 November 2008.
7. Christophe Jaffrelot, 'Abhinav Bharat, the Malegaon Blast and Hindu Nationalism: Resisting and Emulating Islamic Terrorism', *Economic and Political Weekly*, 4 September 2010, p. 52.
8. Ibid.
9. Ibid.
10. Milind Joshirao, spokesperson of Abhinav Bharat; interview done at New Delhi on 18 January 2016.
11. 'Savarkar denies knowledge of plot, refutes charge sheet', *Indian Express*, 23 January 2009.
12. 'Linking AB with Pune blasts highly objectionable: Savarkar', *Indian Express*, 23 February 2010.

13. Charge sheet of Malegaon 2008 blast case, ATS Maharashtra C.R. No. 18/2008, p. 65.
14. Ibid.
15. Ibid.
16. Ibid., p. 66.
17. For details see the confession of Aseemanand, http://www.tehelka.com/2011/01/in-the-words-of-a-zealot/
18. 'The meaning very clearly was, don't get us favourable orders', *Indian Express*, 25 June 2015.
19. 'The importance of being Rohini Salian', *Sunday Express*, 28 June 2015.
20. Charge sheet of Malegaon 2008 blast case, ATS Maharashtra C.R. No. 18/2008, Transcript, pp. 61–72.
21. Ibid., p. 82.
22. Ibid., pp. 88–89.
23. Ibid., p. 90.
24. Charge sheet of Malegaon 2008 blast case, ATS Maharashtra C.R. No. 18/2008, p. 66.
25. Ibid., p. 67.
26. Ibid., p. 68.
27. 'Businessmen under ATS scanner', *Hindustan Times*, 25 November 2008.
28. 'Abhinav Bharat treasurer may have received hawala money', *Times of India*, 10 November 2008.
29. 'Mutalik used Abhinav Bharat funds for business', *Times of India*, 4 February 2011.
30. Ibid.
31. 'Sangh distances itself from Malegaon episode', *Times of India*, 8 November 2008.

32. Christophe Jaffrelot, 'Abhinav Bharat, the Malegaon Blast and Hindu Nationalism: Resisting and Emulating Islamic Terrorism', *Economic and Political Weekly*, 4 September 2010, p. 54.
33. Ibid.
34. 'I masterminded Malegaon blast: Lt Col', *Economic Times*, 7 November 2008.
35. Christophe Jaffrelot, 'Abhinav Bharat, the Malegaon blast and Hindu nationalism: Resisting and emulating Islamic terrorism', *Economic and Political Weekly*, 4 September 2010, p. 55.
36. Ibid.
37. *Indian Express*, 30 October 2008.

7. Bhonsala Military School

1. Christophe Jaffrelot, 'Abhinav Bharat, the Malegaon blast and Hindu nationalism: Resisting and emulating Islamic terrorism', *Economic and Political Weekly*, 4 September 2010, p. 53.
2. 'Purohit's improbable path to becoming a terrorist', *Hindu*, 6 November 2008.
3. Christophe Jaffrelot, 'Abhinav Bharat, the Malegaon blast and Hindu nationalism: Resisting and emulating Islamic terrorism', *Economic and Political Weekly*, 4 September 2010, p. 53.
4. Saikat Datta, 'Godse's War', *Outlook*, 17 November 2008.
5. http://www.rediff.com/news/report/why-terror-probe-must-go-beyond-lt-col-purohit/20120716.htm

6. Christophe Jaffrelot, 'Abhinav Bharat, the Malegaon blast and Hindu nationalism: Resisting and emulating Islamic terrorism', *Economic and Political Weekly*, 4 September 2010, p. 54.
7. Meena Menon, 'Nanded case: of the lost leads and shoddy investigations', *Hindu*, 3 November 2008.
8. Vaibhav Ganjapure, 'Bhonsala school denies training terror suspects', *Times of India*, 1 November 2008.
9. Ibid.
10. 'Swarajya' (Madras), 27 July 1926, in GOI, Home Department (Political), File No. 187/1926, National Archives of India, Delhi.
11. Ibid.
12. Marzia Casolari, 'Hindutva's foreign tie-up in the 1930s', *Economic and Political Weekly*, 22 January 2000, pp. 218, 219.
13. Nehru Memorial Museum and Library, Moonje Papers, Diary 1, Roll 1, pp. 225–227.
14. Ibid., pp. 229–231.
15. Marzia Casolari, 'Hindutva's foreign tie-up in the 1930s', *Economic and Political Weekly*, 22 January 2000, f.n. 6, p. 227.
16. Ibid.
17. Ibid., p. 221.
18. M.N. Ghatate, 'Dr B.S. Moonje – Tour of European Countries', in N.G. Dixit (ed.), *Dharmaveer Dr B.S. Moonje Commemoration Volume, Birth Centenary Celebration 1872–1972*, Centenary Celebration Committee, Nagpur, 1972, p. 69.
19. Nehru Memorial Museum and Library, Moonje Papers, Diary, pp. 23–25.
20. Ibid., pp. 47-48.
21. H.K. Joshi (Appaji), 'Dr Moonje: The Sculptor of Political Life in C.P. & Berar', in N.G. Dixit (ed), *Dharmaveer Dr BS*

Notes

Moonje Commemoration Volume, Birth Centenary Celebration 1872-1972, Centenary Celebration Committee, Nagpur, 1972, p. 34.

22. N.G. Dixit (ed), *Dharmaveer Dr BS Moonje Commemoration Volume, Birth Centenary Celebration 1872-1972*, Centenary Celebration Committee, Nagpur, 1972, p. 7.
23. Pralaya Kanungo, 'RSS's Tryst With Politics', Manohar, Delhi, 2002, pp. 38-39.
24. Nehru Memorial Museum and Library, Moonje Papers, Diary, p. 55.
25. N.G. Dixit (ed), *Dharmaveer Dr BS Moonje Commemoration Volume, Birth Centenary Celebration 1872-1972*, Centenary Celebration Committee, Nagpur, 1972, p. 50.
26. Ibid., p. 60.
27. Pralaya Kanungo, 'RSS's Tryst With Politics', Manohar, Delhi, 2002, p. 51.
28. N.G. Dixit (ed), *Dharmaveer Dr BS Moonje Commemoration Volume, Birth Centenary Celebration 1872-1972*, Centenary Celebration Committee, Nagpur, 1972, p. 69.
29. Major (Retd) Prabhakar Balwant Kulkarni's interview was at Nashik on 21 November 2015.
30. Dr Vivek Raje, Associate Professor, Bhonsala Military College, Nashik; interview done at Nashik on 22 November 2015.

8. Rashtriya Sikh Sangat

1. 'RSS leader Rulda Singh shot at in Patiala', *Tribune*, 30 July 2009.
2. 'Panjab Sikh Sangat leader Rulda Singh dead', *Tribune*, 16 August 2009.

Notes

3. Avinash Jaiswal, National General Secretary (Organization), Rashtriya Sikh Sangat; interview done in Delhi on 9 April 2016.
4. Dr Avtar Singh Shastri, National General Secretary of Rashtriya Sikh Sangat; interview done in Delhi on 9 April 2016.
5. 'BJP's NRI cell to help blacklisted Sikhs', *Times of India*, 18 January 2004.
6. Rajnish Sharma, 'Sikh riots: BJP names figure in records', *Hindustan Times*, 2 February 2002.
7. Ibid.
8. Ibid.
9. Ram Swarup, 'Hindu–Sikh Relationship', Voice of India, Delhi, 1985, p. 4.
10. Ibid.
11. Ibid., p. 5.
12. Ibid., p. 5.
13. Ibid., p. 8.
14. Ibid., p. 15.
15. Ibid., pp. 23–24.
16. Ibid., p. 24.
17. Constituent Assembly Debates, Vol. 10, p. 233. Also available on http://parliamentofindia.nic.in/ls/debates/vol10p7a.htm
18. *Rashtriya Sikh Sangat: An Introduction*, Ludhiana (undated), p. 3.
19. Rajesh Joshi, 'After A Pagan Slur', *Outlook*, 15 January 2001.
20. Ibid.
21. Ibid.
22. 'RSS is just like Aurangzeb', *Outlook*, 15 January 2001.

23. Raghubir Singh, former general secretary of the Rashtriya Sikh Sangat's Punjab unit; interview done at Amritsar on 30 March 2016.
24. The minutes of the Rashtriya Sikh Sangat's Delhi meeting in November 2004 were read out to me by Raghubir Singh, who as its Punjab unit's general secretary was one of the participants.
25. Varinder Walia, 'Yatra had approval of Takht chief: Sangat chief', 26 July 2006, *Tribune*.
26. Ruchika M. Khanna, 'SAD aflutter as RSS spreads wings in Punjab', 12 November 2014, *Tribune*.
27. Sarabjit Pandher, 'Akal Takht sees red in RSS activities,' 19 November 2014, *Hindu*.
28. Ibid.
29. Bhai Mokham Singh, convener, United Akali Dal; interview done at Amritsar on 30 March 2016.

Acknowledgements

This book made it possible for me to work with a number of wonderful people around the country. Some gave me access to information, others helped me overcome the daunting challenges I faced while researching and writing. I wish to express my gratitude to all of them. In addition, my sincere thanks to Rajiv Singh Randhawa, Surender Singh Gharyala, S.M. Mushrif, Shrimant Kokate, Hemant Kulkarni, Sandhya Nare Pawar, Rahul Thorat, Stanley Pinto, Comrade Muneer, Narendra Naik, Asha Naik, Vardesh Hiregange, Phani Raj, G. Rajshekhar, Somnath, Dr K.T. Rammohan, Parameshwaran, Dr Aziz Ahmed, Manoj Kumar, Parvez Parwaz, (late) Anil Sharma, Sanjay K. Jha, Ranjan Thakre, Sherin Varghese, Jitendra Abhar, Digvijaya Singh, Suresh Bhatewra, Subhash Ghatade, D. Umapathy, T.V. Jayan, Niharika Tiwary, Prasoon Kumar Tiwary, Saurabh Lotlikar, Dharmanand Kamat and my editor R. Sivapriya.

There are many other people who helped me with valuable insights and information about the organizations

Acknowledgements

I chose to write about, though only on the condition that they would neither be quoted nor acknowledged. I hope I will be able to thank them in print someday soon without fear that such recognition might bring them harm. They know who they are, and I am grateful to them.

A Note on the Author

Dhirendra K. Jha is a seasoned political journalist who now works with *Scroll*. He is the co-author of *Ayodhya: The Dark Night*, a revelatory account of the installation of the idol of Rama within the Babri Masjid on the night of 22 December 1949.

juggernaut

THE APP FOR INDIAN READERS

Fresh, original books tailored for mobile and for India. Starting at ₹10.

www.juggernaut.in

1

CRAFTED FOR MOBILE READING

Thought you would never read a book on mobile? Let us prove you wrong.

www.juggernaut.in

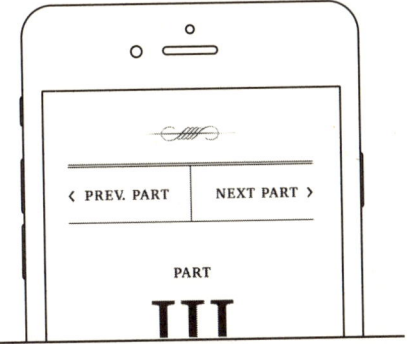

Beautiful Typography

The quality of print transferred to your mobile. Forget ugly PDFs.

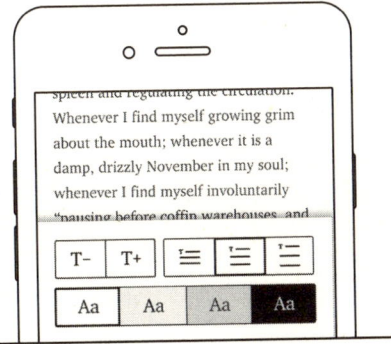

Customizable Reading

Read in the font size, spacing and background of your liking.

www.juggernaut.in

AN EXTENSIVE LIBRARY

Fresh new original Juggernaut books from the likes of Sunny Leone, Twinkle Khanna, Rujuta Diwekar, William Dalrymple, Pankaj Mishra, Arundhati Roy and lots more. Plus, books from partner publishers and all the free classics you want.

www.juggernaut.in

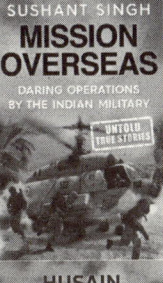

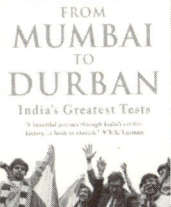

www.juggernaut.in

3

DON'T JUST READ; INTERACT

We're changing the reading experience from passive to active.

www.juggernaut.in

Ask authors questions

Get all your answers from the horse's mouth. Juggernaut authors actually reply to every question they can.

Rate and review

Let everyone know of your favourite reads or critique the finer points of a book – you will be heard in a community of like-minded readers.

Gift books to friends

For a book-lover, there's no nicer gift than a book personally picked. You can even do it anonymously if you like.

Enjoy new book formats

Discover serials released in parts over time, picture books including comics, and story-bundles at discounted rates.

www.juggernaut.in

4

LOWEST PRICES & ONE-TAP BUYING

Books start at ₹10 with regular discounts and free previews.

www.juggernaut.in

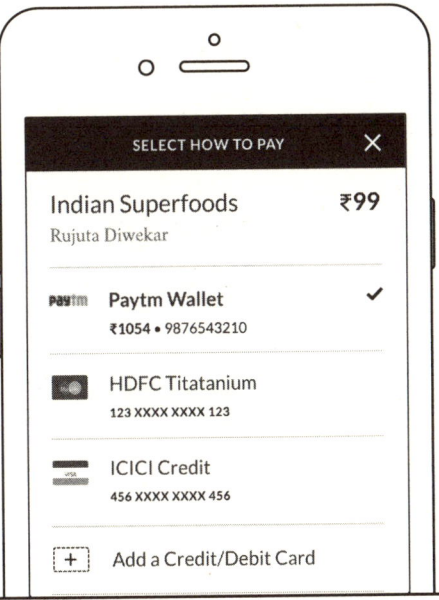

Paytm Wallet, Cards & Apple Payments

On Android, just add a Paytm Wallet once and buy any book with one tap. On iOS, pay with one tap with your iTunes-linked debit/credit card.

Click the QR Code with a QR scanner app or type the link into the Internet browser on your phone to download the app.

SCAN TO READ THIS BOOK ON YOUR PHONE

www.juggernaut.in

DOWNLOAD THE APP

www.juggernaut.in

For our complete catalogue, visit www.juggernaut.in
To submit your book, send a synopsis and two sample chapters to books@juggernaut.in
For all other queries, write to contact@juggernaut.in